THE SHRIVERS' STORY

EYEWITNESSES TO THE BATTLE OF GETTYSBURG

Nancie W. Gudmestad

Published by
SHRIVER HOUSE MUSEUM
Gettysburg, PA

For information contact:
Nancie W. Gudmestad
Director
Shriver House Museum
309 Baltimore Street
Gettysburg, PA 17325
Telephone 717-337-2800
Website: www.shriverhouse.org
Email: mail@shriverhouse.org

ISBN: 978-0-9817751-0-4

First printing: July, 2008
Second printing: March, 2009
Third printing, with revisions: March, 2010
Fourth printing: July, 2011
Fifth printing, with revisions: September, 2016

*This book is dedicated
to the memory of*

*George and Hettie,
Sadie and Mollie*

Contents

Acknowledgements

There are a number of people I would like to thank in connection with writing this book.

First, thanks to my husband, Del, who initially thought the idea of restoring an abandoned house for use as a backdrop to tell the civilian side of the Battle of Gettysburg was a wild notion but was quick to support the idea. Neither of us could have ever known how fortunate we were to select the perfect house in the perfect location.

Thanks to Peg and Leonard Shealer for not selling the house until just the right people came along.

To my big brother, Joe Wilson, who called *every* day to see how the book was progressing and was always there with words of support and encouragement.

To my friends Kim Corradetti and Wendy Allen. Kim, who is passionate about genealogy, never forgets a date once she reads a deed, will or newspaper article and can find any document in minutes. And to Wendy, who so generously shared her amazing computer talents and magic.

To Dr. Marlene Coleman, who happened to sit next to me during a cross-country airline flight, and left me with the conviction that I could do this.

My deepest heartfelt gratitude is due all the tour guides who have passionately shared the Shrivers' story with the thousands of visitors, from all over the world, who have toured the Shrivers' home and heard their incredible story.

And, most importantly, to my friend Harry Conay. Although it has long been my intention to write the Shrivers' story, it was Harry's steadfast encouragement, invaluable advice, unending patience, and long-standing love of history that finally made this book a reality.

Introduction

The smoke had barely cleared over the fields of battle before people began streaming into Gettysburg. At first, hundreds of people arrived every day to search for their wounded loved ones or to locate and identify their dead to bring them home for proper burial. Still others, however, came merely out of curiosity.

Before the events of July 1-3, 1863, people came to this crossroads town primarily to conduct business, to visit family or merely to pass through on their way to Washington, Baltimore, Harrisburg, Pittsburgh or Philadelphia. The new wave of visitors, the first tourists as it were, arrived specifically to see Gettysburg itself, or to be more precise, the blood-stained battlefield they had heard or read so much about.

Reflecting upon the onslaught of visitors, 15-year old Gettysburg resident Tillie Pierce wrote in her book:

> Prior to the battle it was comparatively unknown to the outside world. . . . To-day Gettysburg is a changed place. . . . Scarcely a day passes that does not witness some pilgrimage to this Mecca of loyal devotion to human freedom (Tillie Pierce Alleman. *At Gettysburg, or What a Girl Saw and Heard of the Battle*. New York, W. Lake Borland, 1889, pp. 10, 11. Hereafter cited at Pierce).

This transformation from bucolic whistle-stop to tourist destination was reflected by the *Wagon* Hotel changing its name to the *Battlefield* Hotel.

Among early visitors to Gettysburg was President Abraham Lincoln. A mere four months after the battle, he came to participate in the dedication of the new national cemetery by delivering his immortal *Gettysburg Address*. Both his visit and his speech served to increase the intrinsic, historic value of Gettysburg as a place to visit.

Early visitors not only wanted to see the battlefield, they wanted to take a piece of it home with them. As a result, relic-hunting became popular.

> Visitors soon began to come to see the battlefield, and all wanted relics. We were always on the lookout for bullets and pieces of shell, in fact, anything that could be easily handled to sell to them. We found that a piece of tree with a bullet embedded in it was a great prize and a good seller (Albertus McCreary. "Gettysburg: A Boy's Experience of the Battle." *McClure's Magazine*, vol. 18, no. 33. New York: S.S. McClure Co., July, 1909, p. 243).

Tourists required places to stay while visiting Gettysburg, and, in addition to accommodations provided by established hotels, many visitors were welcomed into the homes of local residents who also served as guides to the battlefield. As they directed the steps of strangers over the still battle-scarred terrain, identifying points of interest, they recounted what they saw and heard before, during and after the battle. The information they imparted was largely militaristic, typically pertaining to the movements of the armies and the placement of various units, to commanders and their strategies, and to particular individuals who distinguished themselves on the field of battle.

Gettysburg became closely identified with the Civil War (often being heralded as the greatest battle of that war), and it remains so identified today as tourists continue to descend upon Gettysburg to discover and to *feel* what took place there. But significant changes have occurred. As the availability of relics and historic artifacts diminished, and such items became valued - and protected - for their historic significance, the manufacture and sale of souvenirs increased to take their place. And just as souvenirs gradually replaced relics, so-called "human interest" stories began to compete for attention alongside heroic military accounts.

Today's tourists want to learn about the Gettysburg *civilians'* experiences as well as the *soldiers'*. How did the typical man, woman and child react to the invasion of their town? Resources specifically addressed to this topic are in short supply. Many hundreds, if not thousands, of volumes have been written about military aspects of the Battle of Gettysburg. Far fewer books, however, have been written about the 2,400 citizens who found themselves embroiled in one of the deadliest and most historic battles ever fought on American soil.

Over the years, the civilian aspect of the battle of Gettysburg has been *largely* (or, at least, *comparatively*) ignored - with two notable exceptions: Jennie Wade (the only civilian killed during the three day battle) and John Burns (an elderly curmudgeon who grabbed his rifle, joined the fray and was wounded in battle). Their oft-repeated accounts have become familiar in the telling, but, arguably, neither is particularly representative of the *other* 2,398 citizens who endured the battle without being killed or without shooting at the invading army.

The Shrivers' Story: Eyewitnesses to the Battle of Gettysburg is the true story of one family who called Gettysburg *home* in 1863. It depicts how not only this battle but the Civil War itself dramatically changed the Shrivers' lives forever. The story of George and Hettie Shriver, although certainly fascinating and unique in its own way, is more typical of the average citizen's, and by extension, provides a fuller picture of the overall civilian experience itself.

Very little was known about the Shriver family prior to the restoration of their house in 1996. To enter the Shrivers' home today, at 309 Baltimore Street, Gettysburg, is to step back in time. Those who walk through all four levels of the house - from cellar to attic and some seven rooms in between - are able to visualize what life was like back in mid-1800, south-central Pennsylvania.

But the Shrivers' story is not solely that of an historic building. More importantly, it is the story of the family who called this house their home. They were a young family with hopes and dreams common to most young families then and now. They dreamed of peace and prosperity, of a safe place in which to raise their family, and for success in their economic endeavors. But the Shrivers' expectations were abruptly interrupted by the coming of the Civil War and by one of the most significant battles of that war. Afterwards, the world as they knew it would never be quite the same. The Shrivers' story is the story of a house and a home, of family and friends, of expectant dreams and intruding realities, of citizens in a time of peace and civilians in a time of war.

The Shrivers' Story
Eyewitnesses to the
Battle of Gettysburg

～～ ～～ ～～

Heavy snow had been falling all day, and frigid winds were blowing hard on the scouting party of approximately eighty men from Cole's Cavalry who were following up on a lead that some of Mosby's guerrillas were in the area of Rectortown, Virginia.

> It was New Year's day, 1864; the thermometer in this mountain country was below zero. The command ran across a large number of Mosby's Cavalry; our scouting party being greatly outnumbered were compelled to fall back, and in crossing Goose Creek, at Leesburg, the men were compelled to swim their horses across the stream, and when they arrived at camp many of the boys were nearly frozen to death. Their heavy boots had gotten full of water which had frozen, and their boots were cut from their feet; A number of the men were compelled to go to the hospital, where it was found necessary to amputate their toes, and in several instances their feet; which had become terribly frostbitten. The command had lost a number of their best men killed and wounded and five or six taken prisoners in this raid (C. Armour Newcomer. *Cole's Cavalry, or Three Years in the Saddle in the Shenandoah Valley*. Freeport, NY: Books for Libraries Press, 1970 reprint of original 1895 ed., pp. 90-91).

One of the men captured in the melee that day was George Shriver of Gettysburg, Pennsylvania.

The Shriver Family

George Washington Shriver

George Washington Shriver was born on July 27, 1836, on his family's large farm located about eight miles southeast of the present-day Borough of Gettysburg, Pennsylvania.

George's great-grandfather, Jacob Schreiber, immigrated to the New World from Germany in the 1730s, settling in Anne Arundel County, Maryland. Lewis P., one of Jacob's nine children, was born in 1750 and after serving in the Revolutionary War, he moved to York County, Pennsylvania, in 1786, the same year James Gettys would lay out plans for his new town, Gettysburg. In 1800 York County was divided into two smaller counties; as a result, the Shrivers now resided in the newly formed Adams County.

Most of Lewis's twelve children would be born in the 36'x20' log cabin he built for the family. The cabin was replaced with a large two-story, Georgian style, stone farmhouse in 1790, on the land he had purchased from the descendants of William Penn. The house was situated deep in the middle of more than 200 acres of rolling central Pennsylvania hillsides. The self-sustaining farm included a small orchard, granary, stone springhouse, large bank barn, grist mill and blacksmith shop; the rich, fertile soil was used for the production of wheat, rye, oats and corn. A weaver's shop, which contained a stitching machine and seven spinning wheels, would attest that there was a modest textile operation as well. Two still-houses produced substantial quantities of gin, rye whiskey and apple brandy. In addition to farming, Lewis's numerous business ventures provided a very comfortable lifestyle for the family.

George's father, George Lewis Shriver, was also a talented businessman, as well as a man of strong faith. As one of the founders of the Elias Evangelical Lutheran Church in nearby Emmitsburg, Maryland, he was one of the first members to be confirmed there. George Lewis Shriver had two sons, Christian and Lewis, who were born to his first wife, Sarah Krise. After Sarah's death, George Lewis married Mary Fisher Rife and together they had three children of their own: Maria Catherine, Isaac and George Washington Shriver. Christian was 17 years old and Lewis was 15 at the time of George's birth; Maria was almost one and a half years old and Isaac had just turned three. George was, thus, the youngest and would be the last child born into the family.

In September, 1852, George's father died suddenly and was buried in the Emmitsburg Lutheran Cemetery. Because Christian, Lewis and Isaac already owned land and operated farms of their own, George inherited the family farm. At sixteen, George was now the man of the house. His father's vast estate included not only a 211 acre farm, barn and distillery, but close to 3,000 gallons of liquor as well.

Less than two miles away from the Shriver farmstead, on the Taneytown Road, lay another very prosperous farm that belonged to Jacob and Sarah (Ickes) Weikert.

Families often tended to be larger in the mid-1800s than they are today, and the Weikert family was no exception. Sarah Weikert bore thir-

Henrietta 'Hettie' Weikert Shriver

teen children: Mary Ann, Isaac, William, Emmanuel, Jacob, Henrietta, George, Sarah Louisa, Julia Ann (lived one month), Levi, Rebecca, Amanda (lived two weeks) and David. Henrietta, born on March 7, 1836, was called *Hettie* from the day she was born.

Since their farms were close to one another, George and Hettie almost certainly knew each other most of their young lives. On January 23, 1855, when they were both eighteen years of age, George and Hettie married at the Weikert farmhouse and immediately started a family of their own.

Their first child, a daughter they christened Sarah Louisa, was named after Hettie's mother and sister. Sadie, as she was called, was

Sadie and Mollie Shriver

born on November 21, 1855. Mary Margaret, nick-named Mollie, came along almost two years later on August 13, 1857. Both girls bore a striking resemblance to their father with beautiful, dark eyes and his strong determined jaw.

On June 4, 1859, George and Hettie's only son was born. Jacob Emmanuel was named after Hettie's father, but he struggled with ill-health from birth. Sadly, less than three months later, Jacob died and was buried in Mount Joy Lutheran Cemetery, a few miles south of the Weikert farm on the Taneytown Road.

∼∼∼ ∼∼∼ ∼∼∼

Located about ten miles north of the border between the Maryland and Pennsylvania state lines, Gettysburg, in the mid-19th century, was a bustling, growing community of 2,400 inhabitants. It was the seat of Adams County and home to two colleges, Pennsylvania College and the Lutheran Seminary. Carriage-making was an important industry, and many folks made their living in the businesses associated with that trade such as tanneries and iron works. There were a number of law offices, three weekly newspapers and numerous shops selling a variety of essential goods. In 1858 the railroad came to town and brought about unlimited business opportunities for those willing to take a chance on using such a *newfangled contraption*. Telegraph service also kept the town up-to-date with what was happening outside Gettysburg. This period of growth and prosperity seemed to present the right time to start a new business within this obviously thriving community.

Shrivers' home on South Baltimore Hill in 1860

On September 8, 1859, George sold 56 acres of his farm for $694.37½ and, in the spring of 1860, paid $290 for a lot-and-a-half of land (a *lot* being 60' of frontage) on Baltimore Street just a few blocks south of the Diamond, a huge open square in the center of

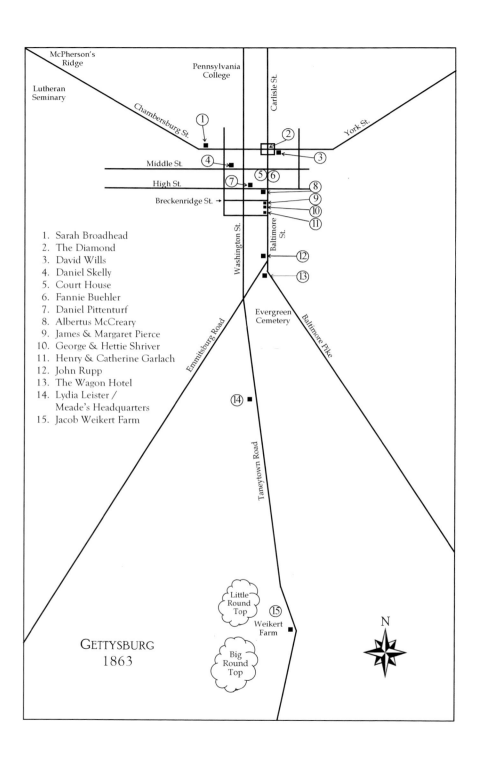

McPherson's Ridge

Lutheran Seminary

Pennsylvania College

Carlisle St.

Chambersburg St.

York St.

① ②

③

Middle St. ④

⑤ ⑥

High St. ⑦

⑧
⑨
⑩
⑪

Breckenridge St. →

Washington St.

Baltimore St.

⑫

⑬

1. Sarah Broadhead
2. The Diamond
3. David Wills
4. Daniel Skelly
5. Court House
6. Fannie Buehler
7. Daniel Pittenturf
8. Albertus McCreary
9. James & Margaret Pierce
10. George & Hettie Shriver
11. Henry & Catherine Garlach
12. John Rupp
13. The Wagon Hotel
14. Lydia Leister /
    Meade's Headquarters
15. Jacob Weikert Farm

Evergreen Cemetery

Emmitsburg Road

Baltimore Pike

⑭

Taneytown Road

Little Round Top

⑮ Weikert Farm

Big Round Top

N

GETTYSBURG 1863

town that was traditionally the hub of all business and social activities. Due to the growth of Gettysburg, the business district around the Diamond was finally extending south down Baltimore Street, and George was going to be part of it. This was the ideal location to build a new home for his growing family and is also where George planned to open his new business: *Shriver's Saloon & Ten-Pin Alley.* The saloon would be located in the cellar of their home, and the backyard was large enough to accommodate a building to house the two-lane ten-pin (bowling) alley. Baltimore Street was one of the town's main thoroughfares, and George's combined enterprise would fit in nicely with the numerous other businesses beginning to appear along the street on the southern end of town.

James and Margaret Pierce were their neighbors to the north, on the corner of Baltimore and Breckenridge Streets. The front, brick portion of their house was built in 1829; a rear addition was added in 1855. It was common practice for people to work where they lived, just as the Shrivers were planning to do. Likewise, the Pierce family not only lived here, but James operated a butcher shop behind the house. Two sons, James and William, worked with their father in the butchering trade while two daughters, Margaret and Matilda (called *Tillie*), attended school and helped their mother take care of the house. Although Mr. Pierce utilized much of his wide lot, 26' of open space remained between his house and the Shrivers' new home.

On the south side of the Shrivers' home was a 60' wide yard which would provide plenty of space for a kitchen garden. While the house was under construction, George planted a small orchard there which would provide cherries, apples, pears and peaches for the family.

The southern edge of the property was bordered by a lot owned by Henry Garlach (pronounced *garlic*). Henry, a carpenter by trade, was well known around town for always wearing his trademark stovepipe hat. He lived here with his wife, Catherine, and their four children: Anna, Will, Katie and Frank. The Garlachs' house was situated on the southern end of their property; Henry operated his cabinet-making business out of a building attached to the north side of their home, closer to the Shrivers.

At the end of the next block, John Rupp operated a tannery business. Across the street from the tannery, at the base of Cemetery Hill, in a fork created where Emmitsburg Road (called Steinwehr Avenue today) splits off from Baltimore Street, sat the Wagon Hotel. Cemetery Hill got its name from the Evergreen Cemetery located at the top of the hill behind the hotel.

≈≈≈ ≈≈≈ ≈≈≈

Built in the Georgian style popular at the time, the Shrivers' two-story, brick home with a wood shingled roof would certainly be one of the finer homes in that section of Baltimore Street. George and Hettie rented a house across the street while their home was being built allowing them to keep a keen eye on the construction process. While George concentrated on business matters, Hettie would have concerned herself with picking out new furniture, paint and wallpaper.

Parlor

Most homes in town had only one small parlor, though some had two, one for receiving guests and one for the family. The

8

Shrivers' plans called for one exceptionally large parlor that occupied the entire north side of the house. It had a fireplace on the north wall, five large windows which made the room especially bright, and one gas lamp. Two windows in the front of the house overlooked Baltimore Street, two in the rear offered a view of the backyard, and one window faced the Pierce house next door.

The wallpaper in the parlor, the most formal room of the Shrivers' new home, had a white background embellished with a 5" marine blue and gold medallion design; against the ceiling was a 3" *Greek key* patterned border, in a matching marine blue and gold, which encircled the entire room.

Used only on special occasions, the parlor is where George and Hettie would receive and entertain family, friends and business associates, and where they would celebrate special family occasions and holidays. When there was a death in the family, it was customary at that time for the funeral to take place at home, with the deceased *laid out* in the parlor.

It was important for children to learn to play a musical instrument, and though Sadie and Mollie would be encouraged to practice the melodeon (a small keyboarded, reed organ) in the parlor and to entertain guests with music and songs, as a rule it was not a room where children would engage in recreation.

The girls would play in the room across the hall from the parlor, the sitting room, which was truly the *heart* of the Shrivers' home. Smaller than the parlor, the sitting room had a gas lamp, as well, and two windows overlooking Baltimore Street. This is where the Shrivers would spend most of their time together as a family. In addition to taking their meals here, they would use the dining table as a workspace for simple household chores such as candlewick trimming and writing letters. The children would use the table to do simple lessons in reading, writing and arithmetic, or they would play with their toys on the floor. George would sit in this room to enjoy a good book or read newspapers to keep abreast of local and national news. Here, too, George and Hettie would enjoy hours playing with the children, reading aloud to them and sharing dreams about their future. There was no fireplace in the sitting room, although a small parlor stove in the corner provided plenty of warmth in the winter; during the summer months the stove could be dismantled and stored in the garret to provide additional space in the sitting room.

Sitting Room

Hettie was probably most excited about her new kitchen and quite proud of the fact that her cook stove was located *inside* her home, not in a separate building behind the house like many other kitchens in town. Six spacious shelves to the right of the fireplace offered plenty of storage space for foodstuffs, crockery, cooking utensils and supplies. The fireplace was there strictly to provide the chimney to vent the cook stove. The wallpaper in the kitchen was a vivid, wildly-patterned, olive green design and the woodwork was painted olive green to match. Once settled in their new home, Hettie would spend many hours here preparing hearty meals for her family, baking bread and pies, churning butter, and canning fruits and vegetables from the garden.

In addition to a view of her garden, two windows overlooking the backyard provided plenty of afternoon sunlight and an unobstructed view of Washington Street, one block away.

Another Gettysburg resident, Fanny Buehler, described her own 1863 kitchen, giving us further insights into what Hettie would likely have had in hers:

> We had stowed away two full barrels of flour, our usual summer supply of hams and lard, we had butter, eggs, coffee, sugar, tea, apple butter, and in our little garden we had onions, some peas, beans, new potatoes, and some old ones . . . (Fannie J. Buehler. *Recollections of the Rebel Invasion and One Woman's Experience During the Battle of Gettysburg.* 1900 reprint of original 1896 ed., p. 20).

What Hettie could not make or grow on her own, such as coffee, tea, spices, rice and other grains, she would purchase from merchants around the Diamond. These items were sold in bulk, scooped out of huge barrels, measured and weighed, and carried home in sacks within her straw basket. Once home, Hettie would transfer the contents of each sack into various clay crocks. If the lid to a crock were ever broken, she would make a replacement using

Kitchen

whatever materials were at her disposal. Often this was a small piece of cloth stretched over the mouth of the crock and tied with cord, but in a pinch, a small flat board could also serve to prevent mice from pilfering and spoiling the crock's contents. For this reason, most households had one or more cats, not primarily as pets, but as *mousers*.

It would be Hettie's responsibility to light the fire in the wood-burning cook stove every morning and to keep the fire going until she got back in bed at the end of each day; maintaining the stove was undoubtedly a full time job. Perhaps one of her most important responsibilities was teaching Sadie and Mollie everything they would need to know about keeping a home when they grew up, married and had homes of their own - just as Hettie's mother had done with her.

It was just a few steps to the garden through the back door in the center hall. Hettie no doubt learned a lot about gardening from her mother and would, in turn, pass down these secrets to a productive garden to Sadie and Mollie. In addition to growing vegetables, fruits, herbs for medicinal and kitchen use, and flowers, Hettie would place a yucca plant in the center of her garden. According to Pennsylvania German folklore, it was customary to plant a yucca in the center of a four-square garden if you were Protestant and a rosemary plant if you were Catholic. As Lutherans, therefore, the Shrivers would likely have a yucca growing in the center of their garden.

The open staircase in the center hall led upstairs to four spacious bedrooms. George and Hettie's bedroom would be simply furnished, the major pieces being a rope bed with a feather mattress, a chest of drawers to accommodate their clothing, a dressing table and a blanket chest for storage.

When the Shrivers were settling into their new home Sadie was five years old and Mollie was three. Their bedroom would contain one rope bed which they would share. Children in the mid-19th century rarely had a bed to themselves and sharing a bed kept them both warmer in the winter. Their bedroom would be filled with

Sadie and Mollie's Bedroom

books and typical girls' toys such as hoops, whirligigs, graces, dolls, tea sets and possibly a Noah's Ark. Those households whose strict religious views forbade playing with non-Biblical toys on Sundays or religious holidays would allow children to play with their Noah's Ark or, as it came to be called, the *Sunday Game*.

With only two children in the family at this point, one of the spare bedrooms would have been used as a guest bedroom. Since George and Hettie both grew up in large families, they would have used this room to accommodate visiting relatives.

Given the absence of closets, which were not common in the mid-19th century, the otherwise unused fourth bedroom would come in quite useful. George could set up a desk in the spare bedroom for a quiet place to work on the details of his new business venture and to keep the books for the household. Hettie would use this spare bedroom to store her sewing supplies and household items she did not need around the house on an everyday basis.

Although her sewing supplies would be stored in the spare bedroom, Hettie would have kept her sewing machine by the window in the center hall to take full advantage of bright, natural sunlight for sewing. The window, overlooking Baltimore Street, also offered a convenient place to keep up-to-date with the neighbors. If Hettie saw someone she knew on the sidewalk in front of her home, she could wave or poke her head out the window to catch up on all the latest news and gossip.

Since there were no bathrooms inside the house, an outhouse was situated at the far southwest corner of the property. Once the fruit trees on the side yard were covered in leaves the outhouse would be hidden from view. Although it would seem like a long walk to the outhouse in the winter, the family would be glad it was that distance from the house when the typically hot, sweltering days of August arrived. Each bedroom was supplied with a large, white ceramic pot with a lid. In the middle of the night, those reluctant to walk outside to the outhouse could remain indoors, within the privacy of their bedroom, to use that *chamber pot*. Traditionally, it was the youngest child capable of doing so whose task it was to empty the chamber pots each morning.

The center hall staircase continued up to the garret, known as an attic today. It was quite a spacious room with a high ceiling that ran the full width of the house. A window at each end of the room provided light and ventilation. This area provided storage for such things as the parlor stove when it was not needed in the sitting room during the summer, the cradle waiting for the next child to be born, or items that were out of season or not frequently needed.

While Hettie would be occupied with furnishing the household, George would be downstairs in the cellar getting the saloon and ten-pin alley ready for operation. Most homes at the time had cellars with very low ceilings and hard-packed dirt floors. But since George's saloon was located in the cellar of his new home, his plans called for unusually high (7½'), horse-hair plastered ceilings; the floor was covered with bricks arranged in a basket-weave pattern.

Down in the cellar, under Hettie's kitchen on the first floor, was another kitchen where meals would be prepared to serve the patrons of the saloon. This kitchen occupied the entire southern half of the cellar and provided plenty of space to store provisions, kegs of liquor and other foodstuffs which would be required in running the saloon. A large fireplace on the south wall had a ten-plate cook stove set just to the front of it. An entrance from Baltimore Street allowed purveyors to deliver provisions directly from the street rather than having to haul their goods around to the back entrance from the garden. Water for use in the kitchen would be brought in from a well in the backyard, but water left over from cooking, laundry or dish-washing could be poured into a sump located in the southeast corner of the cellar floor. The sump, a brick-lined reservoir, drained into a stream that runs under the Shrivers' home and most of the southern end of Gettysburg.

Situated below ground level, the cellar maintained a cool temperature providing the right environment for a root cellar where vegetables could be stored during the winter months. Because there were two kitchens in the house, Hettie may have done some of her sloppier chores, such as making sauerkraut or washing the laundry, in this cellar kitchen. It also provided a more comfortable place to cook in the heat of the summer.

Shriver's Saloon

Shriver's Saloon occupied the northern half of the cellar. Only men would patronize the saloon; they would come to drink, smoke, play checkers, dominoes or cards (possibly even gamble), and discuss the events of the day. It was furnished with a bar, several eating tables with chairs for the patrons, a ten-plate stove for heat, and curtains on the two windows overlooking Baltimore Street at sidewalk level. Since there was no access to the saloon from the street, customers would have entered through the door at the far end of the saloon which faced the backyard. Hettie, or any woman for that matter, would not have wanted patrons parading through her home to access the saloon.

George placed the ten-pin alley in a building located approximately ten feet behind the house, adjacent to the entrance to the saloon. A separate structure covered with wooden clapboard siding, the ten-pin alley stood 14' wide by 65' long. It sat parallel to the northern edge of his property line and was large enough to accommodate two lanes for bowling.

During the construction process George and Hettie honored a longstanding tradition by hiding a shoe in the wall of their new home. Doing so was believed to bring good luck to the family that would live there. They placed a child's shoe (typically the youngest, and therefore probably Mollie's) in the ceiling above the bedroom situated in the northeast corner of their new home. Fortune had been kind to them up to this point, but a little bit of added *insurance* could not hurt.

There were many advantages to living in town. Growing up in the countryside, George and Hettie would have been accustomed to traveling several miles to get to the Diamond to shop and meet friends. But now they lived just three blocks away and could walk there with the girls several times a week to buy whatever they wanted or needed. Hettie could choose from a fine selection of dry goods, china, millinery and dress materials. Once essential errands were completed, it would be a delight to stop at the confectionary store to indulge in candy, cake or an ice cream treat. To them, it must have seemed as if they could buy just about anything just a few steps away from their own home.

~~~ ~~~ ~~~

In the spring of 1861, after a long and cold winter, the fruit trees in the side yard began to bud as Hettie, with the help of Sadie and Mollie, started to work on her new garden.

George sold off the remaining 180 acres of his farm for $3,420. He was twenty-five years old, married with two children, owned a fine home and a business unique to the area and had enough capital to feel secure about his future.

At the same time, important news was coming out of Washington, D.C. Abraham Lincoln had just been elected president and talk of a war between the states, pitting North against South, was heating up. Whether the reason for this friction was due to economics or states' rights, for some the underlying issue was slavery. A small percentage of people in the agricultural South owned slaves; those in the industrialized North generally did not. Also in the South, the average citizen felt a stronger allegiance to his state than to the Federal Union; in the North, it was generally the opposite. Ultimately, people in the southern states felt they were being dictated to by northerners who did not understand them or their way of life. George, who had grown up on a farm less than five miles north of the Mason-Dixon Line, may have felt if the southern states were to secede from the Union, as they threatened to do, and establish a new nation, he would do whatever his country, the United States of America, expected of him in order to defend the Union.

To many northerners, it was inconceivable that all or any portion of the southern states might actually break away to form their own *Confederate States of America*. To do so would be tantamount to a declaration of war. News and speculation about the possibility of war was the talk of the town, but the citizens of Gettysburg, like most of the country, hoped and prayed it would never come to that. Surely another compromise could be achieved to dispel the prospect of war. If war were to erupt, however, everyone in town agreed it would not take very long for the North to defeat the South. Northerners could not imagine that the war - if, indeed, it ever came to be - would last more than a few months at most.

By April, 1861, however, anxiety was mounting throughout the country. After a Confederate attack on Union forces at Fort Sumter, an island just off Charleston in South Carolina, forcing it to lower the American flag and surrender, President Lincoln responded by calling for 75,000 troops to put down the southern rebellion and uphold the Union. The conflict, which everyone had previously dreaded, was now set in motion. The Civil War had begun.

Although George and Hettie probably never talked about these events in front of their children, it is not difficult to imagine the conversations between the two of them after the girls were asleep. Hettie, terrified at the thought of George going off to war, may have pleaded with him to stay home. George, certainly not anxious to get himself killed but feeling it his patriotic duty to enlist, would argue in favor of defending his country. Nevertheless, George remained home that summer to finish and furnish his saloon and ten-pin alley. Upon its completion, with the war still raging, George volunteered for the Union army. Shrivers' Saloon & Ten-Pin Alley would be waiting and ready to open as soon as the war was over and George returned home.

George volunteered for service on August 27, 1861. Less than two weeks later, on September 9th, George was mustered into Cole's Cavalry, Company C in Frederick, Maryland. Maryland, sandwiched between the North and the South, was a so-called *border state* and the loyalties of its citizens were divided. Cole's Cavalry - a Maryland outfit but Union to be sure - was popular with men from northern Maryland and southern Pennsylvania, particularly Adams County.

Even though the saloon was ready for customers, Hettie would not operate the business while George was away. A young woman in the mid-19th century generally did not work outside the home, and a lady of good repute would never dare set foot in a saloon let alone operate one. They were fortunate to have money remaining from the sale of the farm that would provide for Hettie and the children until George returned and the business was running smoothly. In the meantime, Hettie would have to rely on this money and

George's army pay, which was typically sent home to spouses. As a backup, of course, her parents lived just down the road and could be depended upon to assist her if necessary.

Not only was the general consensus that the war would be a short one, but George and Hettie would have held to the belief it would be over by the end of the year. Come Christmas, George would be home and his business would be open; it would be the true beginning of their life together with prospects for a bright future.

Sadly, however, that is not the way things worked out.

December, 1861

George was gone for almost four months and Christmas was fast approaching. In an attempt to maintain a normal lifestyle, houses throughout Gettysburg were decorated with holiday greenery, both inside and out. Countless yards of fresh pine roping and holly decorated doorways and windows. Stockings were hung on mantles, and milk and cookies were set out for a visit from Santa Claus. The Christmas tree, traditionally about 4' tall, would take its place of honor on the table in the center of the parlor. Alternating branches were cut out to form horizontal layers in

The parlor at Christmas

the tree which would then be stuffed with Christmas gifts. The tree would be decorated with strings of popcorn and cranberries, small American flags (to demonstrate one's patriotism during the war), cornucopias filled with candy and nuts, and candles which were generally lit just once - with a big bucket of water nearby in case of an emergency. While many of town's fathers, sons and husbands faced the perils of the Civil War, Christmas day offered a few moments of cheer to help brighten the lives of those loved ones who remained at home. Despite all their hopes that George would spend at least some portion of the holidays with them, Hettie and the girls were disappointed because he did not make it home for Christmas with his family that year.

Christmas day had not quite come to a close when, about 9:30 that evening, a train pulled into the station carrying two battalions (about 800 men) of the newly formed 10th New York Cavalry from Cortland, New York, known as the Porter Guards; they were on their way to the battlefront. Lieut. Henry E. Hayes, of the Porter Guards, later recalled the event:

> They came here filled with the buoyant spirits, the ardent ambition, and the eager hopes of youth. The parting kisses of dear ones left behind were still warm upon their cheeks, the echoes of tearful farewells still trembled in their hearts; but in the firm conviction of duty, and inspired with patriotic devotion to their country, they looked cheerfully forward to a happy reunion of homes as well as of States (*Final Report of the Battlefield of Gettysburg*. Albany: J.B. Lyon, 1900, vol. 1, p. 1158).

As no quarters had been prepared in advance for these soldiers, they slept in the train on Christmas night. Over the next few days, attempts to set up camp were unsuccessful due to the intensely cold weather. Since it was not clear how long these soldiers would stay in the area, the citizens of Gettysburg enthusiastically opened their homes and other buildings throughout town to house them until barracks could be completed. Army correspondent, 2nd Lieu't. John G. Pierce, traveling with the Porter Guards reported in the *Cortland Banner*:

. . . [W]e are now quartered about town in several places, one Company in a Hall, another in a Court House, another in a School House, etc., etc. One Company is pleasantly situated in a Ball Alley, but destitute of balls. The alley is very comfortable, at one end of which once used as a saloon, we have a fire and write letters (where I am now writing this) on an Eating table, undercurtains, for instance as in Barron's. Barracks will soon be furnished, though none are yet erected. Our reception has been the most hospitable . . . (New York, January 9, 1862, p. 1).

Hettie would have gained some satisfaction in housing these men (particularly since they were Cavalry, like George) in the hope someone, somewhere might do the same for George and his comrades if they were in need of a safe, warm place to sleep. It is difficult to image Sadie's and Mollie's reactions to these visitors. Was it exciting for them to see dashing soldiers dressed in new, clean, navy blue uniforms just the way their father looked when he left home? Or was it a bit frightening to see hundreds of soldiers milling about the streets of their town?

Barracks were eventually built to accommodate the Porter Guards, and they remained in Gettysburg until mid-March when they left for their first taste of real battle.

Summer, 1863

Almost two full years passed since George said good-bye to his family; Sadie and Mollie were growing up without their father because he still had not returned from the war. Throughout the month of June, 1863, the people of Gettysburg were filled with questions. Would Confederate General Robert E. Lee really venture north bringing the war to Pennsylvania? Was it true the Rebels were in Chambersburg just a few miles to the west? Were they headed north to Harrisburg? Was it possible the fighting could come to the streets of Gettysburg?

As early as June 15th, Gettysburg resident Sarah Broadhead wrote that she and her neighbors began to "realize the fact that we were in some danger from the enemy, and some persons, thinking the Rebels were near, became very much frightened, though the report was a mistake." In the following days, she speaks of "great fright," "rumors," and "excitement" until, on June 20th, when she writes:

> The report of to-day is that the Rebels are at Chambersburg [about 25 miles west of Gettysburg] and are advancing on here, and refugees begin to come in by scores. Some say the Rebels number from twenty to thirty thousand, others that Lee's whole army is advancing this way. All day we have been much excited (Sarah M. Broadhead. *The Diary of a Lady of Gettysburg, Pennsylvania, From June 15 to July 15, 1863*, p. 6).

In his account, eighteen-year-old Daniel Alexander Skelly recalled those same days:

The month of June, 1863 was an exciting one for the people of Gettysburg and vicinity. Rumors of the invasion of Pennsylvania by the Confederate army were rife and toward the latter part of the month there was the daily sight of people from along the border of Maryland passing through the town with horses and cattle, to places of safety.

Most of the merchants of the town shipped their goods to Philadelphia for safety, as was their habit all through the war upon rumors of the Confederates crossing the Potomac. The merchandising firm in whose employ I had been for a number of years (Fahnestock Brothers) kept a [railroad] car chartered and whenever these rumors reached us, day or night, we packed up the goods and sent it to Philadelphia and went out of business for the time being, until matters became settled again along the border, when the stock was brought back and we resumed our routine (Daniel Alexander Skelly. A *Boy's Experiences During the Battles of Gettysburg*. Self-published, 1932, p. 7).

Another question burned in the minds of the citizens of Gettysburg. Since so many of their men were away fighting, who would protect those who remained behind, many of them women and children? One night a number of the *older* men, deciding it was their responsibility to guard the town from attack, gathered in the Diamond. They resolved if they were going to be soldiers they had to act like soldiers, so they lined up to practice a drill. Tillie Pierce described their exercises in her book:

An amusing incident connected with these reported raids, was the manner in which some of our older men prepared to meet the foe.

I remember one evening in particular, when quite a number of them had assembled to guard the town that night against an attack from the enemy.

They were "armed to the teeth" with old, rusty guns and swords, pitch-forks, shovels and pick-axes. Their falling into line, the maneuvers, the commands given and not heeded, would have done a veteran's heart good. I have often sat and listened to these well-meaning citizens laugh over the contemplation of their comical aspect (Pierce, pp. 18-19).

With their imperfect understanding of how to wage *modern* warfare, and vastly outnumbered as they were certain to be, how could these silver-haired old codgers possibly think they could protect the town if it were ever invaded by an army of seasoned, battle-hardened Confederate forces?

Some of Gettysburg's residents had even more reason to fear such an invasion. Many black families lived just around the corner from the Shrivers, largely concentrated in and around Breckenridge and South Washington Streets. They were especially disturbed by the rumors of Confederates coming anywhere near Gettysburg believing - quite correctly - they would be sent south into slavery if they were spotted and captured. The stories the blacks had heard about slavery were horrible and, since most of them were born free, slavery was a nightmare they did not even dare to imagine. "They regarded the Rebels as having an especial hatred toward them, and believed that if they fell into their hands, annihilation was sure" (Pierce, p. 19).

When rumors flared up, black families could be seen carrying what possessions they could, running down Baltimore Street towards Culp's Hill and the surrounding woods to hide. Tillie Pierce wrote in her book:

> I can see them yet; men and women with bundles as large as old-fashioned feather ticks slung across their backs, almost bearing them to the ground. Children also, carrying their bundles, and striving in vain to keep up with their seniors. The greatest consternation was depicted on all their

countenances as they hurried along; crowding, and running against each other in their confusion; children stumbling, falling, and crying (Pierce, pp. 19-20).

With luck they would find a sympathetic white family to hide them; if need be, however, they would simply live in the hills outside town until such time as they felt it was safe to return.

Hettie and the other citizens of Gettysburg had real reason for concern. On June 26th, a band of Confederate soldiers entered Gettysburg. Fannie Buehler, the Postmaster's wife, lived on Baltimore Street a few blocks north of the Shrivers and across from the Court House, commented on their arrival:

> All through May and June, there were daily, almost hourly reports of raids into Penn'a. . . . At first we were very much frightened by the thought of Rebel soldiers invading our town taking possession of our new Court house and other buildings, and doing all kinds of bad things, such as we read of in the papers. As day by day passed, and they did not come, we lost faith in their coming, and it grew to be an old story. We tried to make ourselves believe they would never come, and we made merry over the reports which continued to be circulated until the really came. When we saw them, we believed (Buehler, p. 6).

> . . . [A]lthough we had been looking for a Rebel invasion for a long time, and had as we thought, prepared ourselves for it; when the Rebels really came, they took us unawares. We were so used to the cry, "the Rebels are coming," when they did not come, were not even in sight, that we paid little or no attention to the daily, even hourly reports, that came to our ears and we even laughed and joked among ourselves, little dreaming they were really so near (Buehler, p. 9).

On the 26th of June they came in considerable force. . . . [T]he infantry were rounding the Square and marching on foot up Baltimore Street, on the same side our house was on . . . so I hurried in, closed the shutters . . . locked the door and buried the keys, and then went to the front door with the children just in time to see "the Rebs" file past and pass on up over Baltimore hill (Buehler, pp. 9-10).

Sarah Broadhead remembered the June 26th incursion this way:

. . . [T]hey came with such horrid yells that it was enough to frighten us all to death. They came in on three roads, and we soon were surrounded by them. We all stood in the doors whilst the cavalry passed, but when the infantry came we closed them, for fear they would run into our houses and carry off everything we had, and went up stairs and looked out of windows . . . . The last regiment stacked arms, on both sides of the street in front of our door, and remained for an hour. They were a miserable-looking set. They wore all kinds of hats and caps, even to heavy fur ones, and some were barefooted. The Rebel band were playing Southern tunes in the Diamond. I cannot tell how bad I felt to hear them, and to see the traitors' flag floating overhead (Broadhead, pp. 8-9).

These early-arriving Confederates were relatively few in number, and after demanding food, clothing, horses and other supplies from the town fathers (which they were denied) departed the very next day. But their presence - and their demands - only increased the fears of townspeople. If this small band of enemy soldiers could demand so very much, what would happen if the entire Rebel army entered the town?

It was late in the morning on the last day of June, a day Hettie would typically spend working in her kitchen. Seemingly out of nowhere a thunderous noise came from the direction of the back-yard. Hettie would be shocked at the sight of thousands of soldiers riding on horseback up Washington Street, a short distance behind her house. Was this, at last, what everyone had feared would happen? Was this everyone's worst nightmare come true? Were these Confederate soldiers? And if so, when they finally came down Baltimore Street, possibly to Hettie's home, would they pillage, plunder, loot and burn? It was the arrival of the Confederate Army that Hettie would have feared most when she saw thousands of soldiers behind her house.

Upon closer inspection, however, these soldiers were not garbed in butternut or gray, but were wearing blue uniforms. These were Union soldiers! And what was most exciting of all was the fact that these men were Cavalry. Could this possibly be Cole's Cavalry? Could George be coming home? Hettie may have run down Breckenridge Street with Sadie and Mollie to join the growing crowd gathering to greet the Union soldiers as they rode into town.

The soldiers which Hettie would have observed, first with consternation and then with relief, were Major General John Buford's division of Cavalry - part of the Army of the Potomac - coming up from Washington D.C. in pursuit of Lee's Army. "I well remember how secure this made us feel. We thought surely now we were safe and the Confederate army would never reach Gettysburg" (Skelly, p. 10).

Nearly everyone in town turned out to welcome the soldiers. The citizens of Gettysburg were so elated they cheered, waved flags and handed out food and water to the weary men as they paraded up Washington Street. People were everywhere - on the sidewalks, in doorways and windows, even up on the rooftops. Hettie's young neighbor, Tillie Pierce, there with a few of her friends, later wrote: "Desiring to encourage them, who, as we were told, would before long be in battle, my sister started to sing the old war song *Our Union Forever*. As some of us did not know the whole of the piece we kept repeating the chorus" (Pierce, p. 29). The men seemed to enjoy this entertainment and, in turn, responded with thanks and cheers.

Buford's troops numbered about three thousand men - more than the number of people living in Gettysburg at the time. It took well over an hour for all the troops to pass by, and almost everyone stayed until the last soldier rode up Washington Street to the northern edge of town where they set up camp in the fields near Pennsylvania College.

All of Gettysburg was excited about the arrival of thousands of soldiers who, it was expected, would now protect them and their town. After weeks of rumors about an impending attack and already having seen small bands of Confederate soldiers in town the folks of Gettysburg would sleep a bit more comfortably this night. At last, with the arrival of Union troops, for the first time in several weeks they were confident that all was now well. However, as they went to bed that night of June 30th, no one in town could have imagined what was in store for them beginning early the next day.

Wednesday, July 1, 1863

With all the commotion surrounding the arrival of troops the day before, Hettie would arise early Wednesday morning, July 1st, to keep as closely as possible to their normal routine so as not to frighten the girls. She was as yet unaware of the fighting that erupted early that morning on the western edge of town. Despite the fact that neither Confederate General Robert E. Lee nor Union Major General George G. Meade desired to fight at Gettysburg (Lee had hoped to capture Harrisburg; Meade had hoped to confront Lee further south in Maryland at Pipe Creek), Confederate Major General Henry Heth's men, moving east from Chambersburg, exchanged fire with Buford's Cavalry in the vicinity of McPherson's Ridge to the west of town. The Battle of Gettysburg had begun.

At first the rolling hills at McPherson's farm prevented the sounds of battle from reaching the southern end of Gettysburg, so people there went about their business as usual. It was mid-morning, however, when the situation began to change. Tillie Pierce recalled:

> It was between nine and ten o'clock, when we first noticed firing in the direction of Seminary Ridge. At first the sound was faint, then it grew louder. Soon the booming of cannon was heard, then great clouds of smoke were seen rising beyond the ridge. The sound became louder and louder, and was now incessant. The troops passing us moved faster, the men had now become excited and urged on their horses. The battle was waging. This was my first terrible experience (Pierce, p. 34).

The low rumbling sound heard in the distance turned into an earth-shaking thunder that must have sounded like a train roaring

33

down Baltimore Street. The deafening noise of the cannons could now be heard all over Adams County. In addition to the tremendous earsplitting sound, the ground shook sending pictures and china crashing to the floor in houses all over the area. People were simultaneously baffled and terror-stricken. Sarah Broadhead aptly described their confusion in her diary:

> I got up early this morning to get my baking done before any fighting would begin. I had just put my bread in the pans when the cannons began to fire, and true enough the battle had begun in earnest, about two miles out on the Chambersburg Pike. What to do or where to go, I did not know. People were running here and there, screaming that the town would be shelled. No one knew where to go or what to do. My husband advised remaining where we were, but all said we ought not to remain in our exposed position, and that it would be better to go some part of the town farther away from the scene of the conflict (Broadhead, pp. 11-12).

Fannie Buehler echoed Broadhead's sentiments:

> My friends urged me to fly with my children to some place of safety in the county, which, by the way, was then nowhere to be found. Officers dashed through the streets ordering everyone to their cellars, as the town would be shelled, people running hither and thither, not knowing what to do or where to go for safety. The battle had commenced (Buehler, p. 17).

After considering her situation, Hettie decided it would be best to leave her house on Baltimore Street and flee to a place of safety, her parents' farm three miles outside of town. She reasoned that, with soldiers fighting *here*, she and her children would be much safer *there*.

Before leaving town Hettie ran to her neighbors, James and Margaret Pierce, next door. No sooner had she stepped outside her front door, than she perceived the noise was even louder outside than it was from inside her house. Not only was it louder, but she could see tremendous clouds of gray smoke filling the sky toward the northwest. At the Pierce's house Hettie pounded on the front door yelling for Margaret. The Pierce's youngest daughter, fifteen-year-old Tillie, later described the encounter this way:

Tillie Pierce

After I had eaten what that day I called dinner, our neighbor, Mrs. Schriver [sic], called at the house and said she would leave the town and go to her father's (Jacob Weikert) . . . . Mr. Schriver, her husband, was then serving in the Union army, so that under all the circumstances at this time surrounding her, Mrs. Schriver did not feel safe in the house.

35

As the battle had commenced and was still progressing at the west of the town, and was not very far off, she thought it safer for herself and two children to go to her parents, who lived about three miles to the south. She requested that I be permitted to accompany her, and as it was regarded a safer place for me than to remain in town, my parents readily consented that I should go.

The only preparation I made for the departure, was to carry my best clothes down to the cellar, so that they might be safe when I returned; never thinking of taking any along, nor how long I would stay (Pierce, pp. 35-36. Tillie spelled Hettie's surname with "c". Refer to "Shriver vs. Schriver" on p. 103 for an explanation.).

Before leaving Hettie asked Mr. Pierce to keep an eye on her home while she was gone. Under the circumstances, he said, he would do the best he could.

Hettie ran back to her home with Tillie just a few steps behind. She called to her children and without another moment's hesitation, around one o'clock in the afternoon, Hettie, Sadie, Mollie and Tillie started for the Weikert farm. In their haste to leave town, Hettie took a shortcut through Evergreen Cemetery where they passed countless soldiers focused on getting cannons ready to fire. Several soldiers stopped, momentarily, warning Hettie to find a place to hide telling her she was putting herself and her children in great danger. Hettie, determined to get to her family's farm, ignored their well-intentioned warnings and continued down the Taneytown Road which was filled with wagons, horses and soldiers as far as they could see.

As I looked toward the Seminary Ridge I could see and hear the confusion of the battle. Troops moving hither and thither; the smoke of the conflict arising from the fields; shells bursting in the air, together with the din, rising and falling in mighty undulations . . . .

We soon reached the Taneytown road, and while traveling along, were overtaken by an ambulance wagon in which was the body of a dead soldier. Some of the men told us that it was the body of General Reynolds, and that he had been killed during the forenoon in the battle (Pierce, p. 39).

Over the previous several days it had rained quite heavily and the roads were deep with mud. With each step the heavy muck oozed over the tops of their shoes, and the hems of their dresses were caked with mud making it even more difficult to walk.

While they were still about a mile and a half from the Weikert farm - in other words, about half way between the farm and home - they were engulfed by thunderous noise and surrounded by chaos. The road was so muddy it seemed almost impossible to continue when they reached a small farmhouse on the side of the road. Tillie described their situation: "While we were standing at the gate, not knowing what to do or where to go, a soldier came out and kindly told us he would try to get some way to help us further on, as it was very dangerous to remain there" (Pierce, p. 40).

The farmhouse, belonging to Lydia Leister, was one Hettie passed countless times on prior occasions during trips in and out of town, to and from her parents' farm. A short time later the same soldier returned and said they should hurry back to the road. He had stopped a wagon and convinced the driver that, even though his wagon was quite full, he should take the four ladies the remainder of the way down Taneytown Road to the Weikert farm. Once again, they struggled through the deep mud to reach the wagon, thanking the soldier who had helped them as the wagon drove away. Tillie wrote:

> The mud was almost up to the hubs of the wheels, and underneath the mud were rocks. The wagon had no springs, and as the driver was anxious to put the greatest distance between himself and the battle in

the least time possible, the jolting and bumping were brought out to perfection (Pierce, pp. 40-41).

The wagon passed scores of Union soldiers, other wagons, cannon, caissons, artillery and more on route to battle. Surrounded by the sights and sounds of war, it was a frightening ride. The trek to her father's farm had never before seemed so far, so long or so terrifying.

The wagon finally reached the Weikert farm and the familiar gray stone farmhouse surrounded by a white picket fence where Hettie grew up. Jumping off the wagon they ran to the house which sat on a small knoll just a few yards off the western edge of the road. Here, three miles from town and with her family, Hettie felt they would all be safe.

Home of Jacob and Sarah Weikert (c.1880s)

Jacob and Sarah Weikert

A large bank barn stood to the left of the gravel lane leading from the Taneytown Road. A carriage house and several small outbuildings sat between the barn and the farmhouse on the right. Sprawling open fields behind the house were bordered by two large hills less than a hundred yards to the west. While growing up on the farm, the Weikert children had spent many pleasant hours exploring those fields and crawling through every crevice created by the massive boulders covering the hills. From the top of the hills, one could seemingly see forever - Gettysburg was clearly visible to the north and the South Mountains to the west. The two hills on the western edge of Jacob Weikert's property were known as the Roundtops; today they are more commonly known as Big Round Top and Little Round Top!

On Taneytown Road, there appeared to be no end to the steady stream of Union troops and artillery passing the Weikert farm heading into Gettysburg.

It was indeed a thrilling sight. How the men impelled their horses! How the officers urged the men as they all flew past toward the sound of the battle! Now the road is getting all cut up; they take to the fields, and all is an anxious, eager hurry! Shouting, lashing the horses, cheering the men, they all rush madly on.

Suddenly we behold an explosion; it is that of a caisson. We see a man thrown high in the air and come down in a wheat field close by. He is picked up and carried into the house (Pierce, p. 41).

It was obvious they would soon be faced with countless hungry soldiers, many of them wounded, so Mrs. Weikert, Hettie and the others started baking biscuits and making beef tea in the cellar kitchen. With all the commotion of war surrounding them, this was a much safer location than the upstairs kitchen.

Tillie sought some way to be useful; after watching countless hot, weary soldiers pass by the farmhouse on their way into town she knew what she had to do. For the next several hours Tillie stood by the side of the road passing out water to the never ending column of men double-timing it down Taneytown Road. The men would grab a tin cup, take a quick gulp or two, then throw the cup on the side of the road for Tillie to refill so others could thus imbibe.

As they had anticipated, an endless procession of wounded soldiers began to arrive. Men were walking, limping, some crawling and many were carried to the Weikert farm. They were bleeding, burnt, bandaged and some were blinded or missing limbs. All but the most severely wounded begged for water. Many cried aloud for their loved ones and for someone, *anyone*, to write a note conveying their final goodbyes. When they thought there could not possibly be any more wounded men out there, even more would arrive.

Tending to the wounded was extremely difficult; these citizen caregivers - most of whom were female - were not used to the incredible horrors they saw. Tillie described a wounded soldier being carried into the house: "As they pass by I see his eyes are blown out and his whole person seems to be one black mass" (Pierce, p. 41). Later, in an ironic comparison between his loss of sight and the horrors to which she is introduced, Tillie added,

"How terribly the scenes of war were being irresistibly portrayed before my vision" (Pierce, p. 42).

Evening fell and the sound of gunfire and cannons began to wane, signaling that even more men would be arriving in search of food and a place to bring the wounded. By nightfall the house and barn were filled with dead, dying and wounded men.

Hettie, her mother and her sisters worked in the sweltering kitchen listening to a variety of sounds that came drifting into the house through the open windows. The sounds of men talking and the non-stop chopping of wood needed to feed the many campfires mingled with the sounds of young boys and men wailing in misery and calling for loved ones as some fought an often futile battle to stay alive.

Drawn by sounds coming from the yard, Hettie's younger sister, nineteen-year-old Beckie, walked out to the barn with Tillie who wrote: "Nothing before in my experience had ever paralleled the sight we then and there beheld. These were the groaning and crying, the struggling and dying, crowded side by side, while attendants sought to aid and relieve them as best they could" (Pierce, p. 44). Shocked and frightened by what they had just witnessed the girls ran back to the farmhouse in tears. What they did not realize, though, was that this scene would be replayed before them, over and over again, in the days and weeks to come. These were sounds they would hear in nightmares for the rest of their lives. Indeed, these would be days none of them would ever forget.

As particularly horrific as this battle seemed to them (and given their civilian ignorance of war, they really had nothing with which to compare it), they were dismayed to hear, at the end of the day, many Union soldiers sharing similar views. Soldiers reported that the battle was like nothing they had seen before, and over the past few years they had certainly seen plenty. They said the number of wounded and dead was staggering and they were fearful the Rebels might actually prevail. Over the past two years the Union army had lost more than a few battles to forces commanded by Robert E. Lee, but these were on southern soil. While it was difficult enough to lose *any* battle, to be defeated by the Confederates on Union soil, here at Gettysburg, would be particularly humiliating!

Thursday, July 2, 1863

Early on the morning of July 2nd, the Weikert family watched from the front porch as the procession of Union soldiers filing past the house toward town continued, non-stop, for hours on end. The women, once again, fired up the cook stoves and continued to cook.

> During the whole of this afternoon Mrs. Weikert and her daughters were busy baking bread for the soldiers. As soon as one ovenful was baked it was replenished with new, and the freshly baked loaves at once were cut up and distributed. How eagerly and gratefully the tired-out men received this food! (Pierce, p. 52).

And, just as they had done the day before, the younger girls carried water from the spring to the road for the men to drink as they hurried by. Much to Jacob Weikert's dismay the spring eventually ran dry, so the girls started taking water directly from his well instead.

Tillie abandoned her post long enough to share some exciting news. With a tin cup still in the grip of her hand, she flew into the kitchen to tell everyone how she had given water to an honest-to-goodness, real general. General George Meade, head of the entire Army of the Potomac, had stopped on the road in front of the Weikert farmhouse and took a drink from Tillie's cup! Or so she had been told and always believed.

Tillie was still reeling with excitement when an officer knocked on the kitchen door asking Mrs. Weikert's permission for him and several other soldiers to go to the roof in order to get a view of the fields behind the house. Since Mrs. Weikert was too busy to accompany them, she asked Tillie to do so. The men followed Tillie up the stairs and she showed them the trap door to the roof. The soldiers opened the trap door and conferred with one another as they took turns gazing through their field glasses at the thousands of men moving around the countryside. When she returned to the kitchen, Tillie was even more excited than before because one of the soldiers had allowed her to look through his field glasses. The thick smoke and dust from the movement of countless numbers of soldiers and horses made it difficult for her to see clearly but Tillie described the scene:

> The country for miles around seemed to be filled with troops; artillery moving here and there as fast as they could go; long lines of infantry forming into position; officers on horse-back galloping hither and thither! It was a grand and awful spectacle and impressed me as being some great review (Pierce, pp. 51-52).

Because of the constant gunfire surrounding them, family members tried to stay away from the windows as they worked inside the house. Occasionally risking a peek, however, they could spy the bodies of dead Union soldiers, shot by Confederate sharpshooters, lying in the yard behind the house. These bodies had to lie in the grass under the hot summer sun for hours, because at this point it was much too dangerous for the other soldiers to retrieve their fallen comrades.

The loud, thunderous sound of rifles and cannons firing for hours on end made communication difficult if not impossible. As Hettie and the others worked side by side in the kitchen, their voices became hoarse from trying to shout over the constant din to exchange even just a few necessary words of instruction, consolation or encouragement. Despite the thick stone sheltering walls, the farmhouse shook and their throats and ears ached.

> Toward the middle of the afternoon heavy cannonading began on the two Round Tops just back of the house. This was so terrible and severe

that it was with great difficulty we could hear our-selves speak. It began very unexpectedly; so much so, that we were all terror-stricken, and hardly knew what to do (Pierce, p. 53).

In the middle of the afternoon there was a brief and eerie silence. Then, suddenly, the explosion of cannon fire seemed to be louder - if that were possible - than any they had heard before. Soldiers were scrambling for cover and shouted to the family that everyone should leave the Weikert farmhouse immediately because it was no longer safe to remain there. With massive explosions in the air over their heads, and in compliance with the order, they immediately dropped what they were doing and raced across an open field to a neighboring farmhouse about a half-mile away. As they fled they could not help but look toward town.

On our way over, my attention was suddenly attracted, in the direction of the town, to what seemed a sheet of lightning. This light remained in the sky quite awhile. The first thought that flashed upon my mind was, perhaps it is Gettysburg burning . . . (Pierce, p. 53).

Suddenly, Mrs. Weikert stopped as abruptly as if she had run into an invisible wall. A lively discussion ensued between her and Mr. Weikert, after which he turned and hurried back towards their home. Mrs. Weikert then ran as fast as she could to catch up with the others.

After reaching the farmhouse, frightened and out of breath, they were told by soldiers at that location they should go back to where they had just come from; cannon shells firing over the Round Tops were more likely to overshoot their mark, passing harmlessly over the Weikert farmhouse, to land *here* instead! Assuming the soldiers knew best, the small crowd of people, who had just barely caught their breath, turned and ran back across the field to the Weikert farmhouse.

Upon returning home, exhausted from two sprints across the rugged, uneven field, they learned why Mr. Weikert had been sent back to the house by his wife. Mrs. Weikert wanted Jacob to retrieve her brand new, quilted petticoat. Obviously, this was much too important an item to leave behind - even in the midst of a battle!

> During the whole of this wild goose chase the cannonading had become terrible! Occasionally a shell would come flying over Round Top and explode high in the air over head . . . . It seemed as though the heavens were sending forth peal upon peal of terrible thunder directly over our heads, while at the same time, the very earth beneath our feet trembled (Pierce, pp. 55-56).

Despite the cannon shot passing over and exploding beyond - but still quite near - their home, the women immediately went back to the kitchen to continue cooking. They headed straight for the cook stove to check on several pans of bread they had placed in the oven shortly before leaving the house earlier that day. The ladies were happy to learn the bread had not burned, which they had feared, because soldiers had taken the pans out of the stove in time. The soldiers smiled broadly as they confessed having enjoyed every bite.

This day continued just like the day before with the ladies baking as much and as fast as they could and tending to the wounded; the children helped by tearing cloth into bandages.

Late in the afternoon soldiers gathered outside the farmhouse could be heard saying the Rebels were on *this* side of the Round Tops and were headed in their direction. Shouting through an open window, the soldiers informed the Weikert family it would prove to be disastrous for the Union army if these Rebels managed to succeed in their effort to reach the Taneytown Road. Sure enough, as the family looked out the windows they saw Confederate soldiers heading in their direction.

At just about that same moment, from not too far off, the sound of fife and drum could be heard in another direction. Everyone now ran to the windows on the opposite side of the house, thrilled at the sight of the Pennsylvania Reserves coming around the barn! This was regarded as one of the most beautiful sights they had ever seen. A short skirmish ensued until the Confederates were driven back toward Little Round Top, but not before several of their men were killed directly behind the farmhouse.

As the sun set, the number of wounded soldiers, once again, continued to grow. Since the barn, house and outbuildings were already spilling over with wounded, new arrivals were placed wherever space permitted on the ground surrounding the farmhouse.

> On this evening the number of wounded brought to the place was indeed appalling. They were laid in different parts of the house. The orchard and space around the buildings were covered with the shattered and dying, and the barn became more and more crowded. The scene had become terrible beyond description (Pierce, p. 58).

Friday, July 3, 1863

The next morning they woke to another muggy day, though it looked as if the sun were trying to come out. Not too far off in the distance the sound of battle began anew. "Already there was occasional musketry and cannonading in the direction of Gettysburg, and we expected greater danger than at any time before" (Pierce, p. 69).

By now everyone in the Weikert farmhouse had become somewhat accustomed to the constant shaking of furniture and rattling of windows caused by the reverberations from nearby cannon fire. Relatively unfazed, they simply continued working, scraping together what little food they could find to prepare breakfast for the family. They were nearly finished cleaning up the breakfast dishes when Tillie came downstairs, no doubt having overslept due to the excitement and subsequent exhaustion of the day before. As she walked across the kitchen, Tillie looked out the window and was startled by the sight of soldiers setting up cannons just outside the farmhouse. Everyone in the kitchen had been so busy they did not take notice of this until now. Recognizing that the placement of cannons so near to the house meant the fighting that was anticipated would be equally close, everyone retreated to the cellar, both to hide and to continue cooking in the fireplace there.

After two full days of fighting, the Weikert farm was devastated. The farmland was ravaged by thousands of soldiers marching over it on foot or by wagon, every fence was torn down to use for camp fires and all the crops were gone. In addition, the house was being used as a hospital; surgery was taking place in almost every room; most of the linen and cloth were confiscated for bandages; bedding was taken for use by the soldiers; and all the meat, flour, rice and Sarah Weikert's entire stockpile of canned fruits and vegetables were gone.

Jacob Weikert was dismayed to learn that, because his spring had already run dry, soldiers were now taking water directly from the well. Mr. Weikert was concerned, rightly so, that given the unprecedented demand for fresh water imposed by the necessities of war, his well might also run dry. There was no way of knowing how long the conflict would go on, and Jacob, as head of the household, was enduring an enormous amount of stress trying to protect his family.

Lieut. Ziba B. Graham of the 16th Michigan Infantry reported:

> On my way back to rejoin the regiment I called at a large [Weikert] house for a drink of water; I saw that the well crank had been removed. I turned to a rebel captain who was lying on the grass and asked him if he knew where it had gone to; he said that but a few moments before the owner of house had taken it off, declaring he was not going to have his well pumped dry by rebel soldiers, and that they wasted the water. This captain begged that I might get it again. There were some fifty rebel wounded in the yard, besides a few of our own men . . . I went into the house, found this man [Mr. Weikert], a mean Dutchman buried in the bosom of his family, and his family buried in the bowels of the cellar, they having taken safe refuge from the hail of iron which was bursting in every direction. I ordered him to give up the well crank. He first refused. Just at that time a shell struck his chimney, and the noise and rattle of the falling brick nearly frightened him to death. I threatened to shoot him if he did not give me the crank; this brought it out of its hiding place back of the stairway. I went out, watered the boys, put two of the least wounded in charge of it and then left, receiving the thanks of all (On To Gettysburg: Ten Days From My Diary of 1863, p. 13 as accessed from www.gdg.org/Research/ MOLLUS/mollus15.html on October 19, 2007).

Mr. Weikert regarded water as an important commodity, one which he had freely shared until now. Fearing his water supply would run dry, knowing their entire livelihood as a farm family depended on it, and affected by the extraordinary circumstances of war, Mr. Weikert apparently overreacted. And so, in addition to all his other losses, it now appeared that he would lose yet another: his water.

Before long a young soldier explained to Mr. Weikert that it was reported the Rebels were making another effort to come over the Round Tops; if they succeeded in doing so, the house and the family would be in the midst of intense and bloody combat. The soldier advised that, once more, it would be best for the family to leave. With the sound of gunfire so near, and prompted by this new report, no one wasted any time heading for the carriages. As they ran to the barn, a shell flew over their heads with a loud whistle hastening their escape even further.

Without wasting a moment, they boarded the carriages and started for what they hoped would be a place of greater safety. They drove their carriages south on Taneytown Road for about a mile, then made a left turn, heading toward Baltimore Pike to a small town called Two Taverns. No one spoke as they were anxious to get out of harm's way. The sound of gunfire diminished the further they rode away from the Weikert farm. Once they were a comfortable distance from the farm, they felt confident for the first time in three days that they were out of harm's way.

Approaching a small band of Union soldiers, Mr. Weikert stopped to talk to one of them standing by the side of the road. This soldier informed Mr. Weikert that there had been a fierce cavalry engagement at this very location just an hour earlier. A short distance from the road they could see a large field filled with Rebel prisoners. These were the first of countless Confederate prisoners Hettie and the others would see in the days to come. It was difficult not to feel sorry for these unfortunate men who looked disheveled and exhausted; many appeared to be in a state of shock.

While Mr. Weikert was talking to the Union soldier, another young man in blue, eating a piece of hardtack, struck up a conversation with Tillie who was sitting in the back of the wagon.

Tillie had not eaten anything since dinner the previous evening, and she had missed breakfast this morning, so she must have appeared famished. The soldier reached into his haversack and offered her a piece of hardtack. Tillie was surprised, thanked him and took a bite. "I accepted it with thanks, and nothing that I can recall was ever more relished, or tasted sweeter, than that Union soldier's biscuit, eaten on July 3, 1863" (Pierce, p. 71). Not many (if indeed, *any*) Civil War soldiers would have agreed with Tillie's favorable opinion of hardtack!

They left the soldiers and traveled to a farmhouse a safe distance from the fighting. It appeared they were not the only folks to leave Gettysburg, because this house was crowded with others who had had the same idea. Friends and strangers alike spent the day together, refugees from a battle they never imagined would take place in their town.

The sound of the battle resonated throughout the hillsides for several more hours. Late in the afternoon the noise began to subside, much earlier in the day than it had on the previous two days. The prolonged quietude was eerie. It remained silent for a very long time before everyone finally agreed it was probably safe for all the families to return to their homes.

Jacob and Sarah Weikert, Hettie, Sadie and Mollie, Beckie and Tillie - all the folks who had left the Weikert farm house earlier that morning - began piling back into the carriages for the return journey. The closer they got to the farm, the harder it was to comprehend what they saw. Unlike anything they might have expected, the entire countryside was in disarray.

> As we drove along in the cool of the evening, we noticed that everywhere confusion prevailed. Fences were thrown down near and far; knapsacks, blankets and many other articles, lay scattered here and there. The whole country seemed filled with desolation (Pierce, p. 71).

After a long, slow ride they finally reached the Weikert farm. Approaching the farmhouse, everyone drew a deep breath as the horses slowed to a stop in the middle of Taneytown Road. They stared in disbelief. What appeared to be dark blankets scattered on the ground as far as they could see were, upon closer examination, innumerable lifeless men and horses. The motionless, humid summer air was heavy with the smell of gunpowder. Scores of men were wounded and crying out in agony; quite a few were already dead. "Upon reaching the place I fairly shrank back aghast at the awful sight presented. The approaches were crowded with wounded, dying and dead. The air was filled with moanings, and groanings" (Pierce, pp. 71-72).

The gravel lane leading to the farmhouse was so cluttered with bodies and debris it was impossible to drive the carriages back to the barn. Slowly, one by one, they got off the carriages which were still standing in the middle of Taneytown Road. As they walked to the farmhouse, entering a maze of fallen soldiers lying on the ground, they had to control each footstep so as not to tread on any of them.

Entering the farmhouse, they were further stunned by what they saw inside. The house was overflowing with wounded soldiers, many hideously so. Once the officers realized these were the Weikerts returning to their home, they graciously cleared the house of those wounded soldiers capable of being moved in order to give the family a little space and privacy. Despite everything they had seen and heard over the last few days, Hettie and her family found themselves in a state of disbelief, not sure where to begin. They quickly realized they needed to get back to work.

Hettie got started in the kitchen trying to make what little food was left stretch as far as humanly possible. Mrs. Weikert dashed through the house looking for any remaining fabric - sheets, curtains, tablecloths, even clothes - that could be torn into bandages for the surgeons

Doctors set up all manner of tables to treat the wounded soldiers. Surgeons used benches, barrels covered with wooden planks, doors taken right of their hinges, even the Weikerts' kitchen table - anything at all upon which they could do their grisly work. The family watched in horror as wounded men, crying in anguish, were carried to these makeshift operating tables. While amputation was undoubtedly necessary to save lives, it was still a shocking experience for the onlookers.

> By this time, amputating benches had been placed about the house, I must have become inured to seeing the terrors of battle, else I could hardly have gazed upon the scenes now presented. I was looking out one of the windows facing the front yard. Near the basement door, and directly underneath the window I was at, stood one of these benches. I saw them lifting the poor men upon it, then the surgeons sawing and cutting off arms and legs, then again probing and picking bullets from the flesh (Pierce, pp. 72-73).

Once a wounded soldier was placed on an operating table, someone would administer a little chloroform to put the patient to sleep.

> But the effect in some instances was not produced; for I saw the wounded throwing themselves wildly about, and shrieking with pain while the operation was going on.
>
> To the south of the house, and just outside of the yard, I noticed a pile of limbs higher than the fence. It was a ghastly sight! Gazing upon these, too often the trophies of the amputating bench, I could have no other feeling, than that the whole scene was one of cruel butchery (Pierce, pp. 73-74).

It was obvious, even to a novice, that some of these men were so badly wounded there was no hope of their survival. These were the men that were the most difficult to face. To make matters even worse, doctors and their assistants wore aprons soaked in blood which was splattered everywhere. After an unending succession of patients, blood formed crimson puddles on the ground beneath their feet. As appalling as this sight must have been for Hettie and the other adults, one can only imagine what the impact must have been on little seven-year-old Sadie and five-year-old Mollie. Nothing in their young lives could have ever prepared these two small children for the horrific sights and sounds they personally experienced.

Everyone worked late into the night doing whatever it took to relieve the pain and suffering of as many wounded men as possible. The soldiers did offer one bit of hope, though; they were filled with confidence that they had turned back the Rebels - but at what price?

Tomorrow was the Fourth of July; for Hettie and the others, there would be no traditional picnics this year.

Saturday, July 4 –
Monday, July 6, 1863

After three long days of battle, the early morning silence was broken, not with the rumble of cannon fire but with cry of victory. Despite the events of the past several days, the Fourth of July was never celebrated with such lively fervor as it was that summer. Resounding cheers could be heard coming from all directions. Even some of the most severely wounded men found a reason to smile.

> On the summits, in the valleys, everywhere we heard the soldiers hurrahing for the victory that had been won . . . . Most befitting was it, that on the fourth of July, an overruling and all-wise Providence should again declare this people, free and independent of the tyranny upheld by an enemy . . . . We were all glad that the storm had passed, and that victory was perched on our banners . . . . But oh! The horror and desolation that remained. The general destruction, the suffering, the dead, the homes that nevermore would be cheered, the heart-broken widows, the innocent and helpless orphans! Only those who have seen these things, can ever realize what they mean (Pierce, pp. 75-76).

This is how Daniel Skelly described that July 4th from his vantage point in town:

> About 4 A.M., there was another commotion in the street, this time on Baltimore . . . It seemed to be a noisy demonstration. Going hurriedly to the win-

dow I looked out. Ye gods! What a welcome sight for the imprisoned people of Gettysburg! The Boys in Blue marching down the street, fife and drum corps playing, the glorious Stars and Stripes fluttering at the head of the lines (Skelly, p. 19).

Similarly, Fannie Buehler, who was in her home in town, wrote:

All around us were evidences of a great battle. The wounded, the dead and dying, all heaped together; horses that had fallen beneath their riders, with limbs shattered and torn - dead, wounded and bleeding - broken down artillery wagons, guns and knapsacks, cartridge boxes, capes, coats and shoes; indeed all the belongings of a soldier, and the soldier himself, all lying in the streets, so far as we could see, either up or down. Such was the awful scene spread out before us, as we ventured to the front of our house on the morning of the 4th of July, 1863 (Buehler, pp. 24-25).

For the next several days work went on around the clock at the Weikert farm, everyone settling into a routine of cooking and taking care of the wounded. No matter how tired they were, there was always one more soldier who needed help. Ovens never cooled and the wounded were treated until they could be moved to one of the hospitals hastily set up around the area.

During this time many a brave and noble spirit went from its tenement, and passed to the great beyond. This is what it meant, when they silently carried out a closed rough box, place it upon a wagon and drove away (Pierce, pp. 76-77).

On July 5th, Hettie's younger sister, Beckie, her beau, Lieut. George Kitzmiller, and Tillie walked through the fields behind the Weikert farmhouse to the top of the hill called Little Round Top.

The sights they saw there were similar to what Fannie Buehler had seen in town the day before.

> The view there spread out before us was terrible to contemplate! It was an awful spectacle! Dead soldiers, bloated horses, shattered cannon and caissons, thousands of small arms. In fact everything belonging to army equipments [sic], was there in one confused and indescribable mass (Pierce, p. 81).

The first few days after the battle would be looked back upon as a hazy blur of activity. Civilians and soldiers worked side by side assisting surgeons, cooking, nursing, collecting and dispensing water, wrapping bandages and writing letters to loved ones; they did anything they could to comfort the wounded and dying. The task was so overwhelming even children were called upon to help.

Ten-year-old Sadie Bushman lived just around the corner from the Shrivers, on Breckenridge Street. Recollecting her experiences, she later wrote:

> As I reached the hospital tent, a man with a leg shattered almost to a pulp was carried in. 'Give him a drink of water while I cut off his leg' was the command I got. How I accomplished it, I do not know, but I stood there and assisted the surgeon all through the operation (San Francisco *Bulletin*. March 9, 1902, from the collection of the Adams County Historical Society).

The same scene was repeated day and night, not only at the Weikert farm, but in homes, churches, warehouses, barns and various other make-shift hospitals throughout Gettysburg and the surrounding countryside. It was not long before the stench from thousands of dead men and animals began to saturate the humid summer air.

Tuesday, July 7, 1863
and Thereafter

It was seven days since the onset of the battle and the Weikert farm was barely recognizable. Like many other residents of Gettysburg who suffered property damage, Jacob filed a claim with the Quartermaster General's Office seeking monetary restitution for his losses:

12 Acres Wheat, 15 bu. per Acre, @ $2.50 per bu.	$450.00
16 Acres Meadow, 1½ tons pr. acre, @ $24 per ton	576.00
11 " Oats, 35 bush per acre @ $1.00 pr bushel	385.00
6 " Corn, 60 " " " @ $1.00 " "	360.00
3500 Rails, @ $11.00 per hundred, large logs	385.00
Cutting roads and otherwise injuring place	500.00
Cutting young timber from 30 Acres woodland	100.00
	$2,756.00

Jacob Weikert also requested compensation for "bed clothing, pillows, sheets, Coverlets, Clothing and underclothing taken, Kitchen furniture, tin and table ware" (Records of the Quartermaster General's Office, Miscellaneous Claims, Book M, #521).

Jacob Weikert's claim was handled as rapidly as the claims of everyone else in Gettysburg who filed for damages - very slowly. The Quartermaster General's Office denied his requests on numerous occasions claiming Jacob did not have receipt vouchers or the testimony of any former officers knowledgeable of the facts in his situation. After more than eleven years of attorneys' fees, correspondence and rejection letters, Jacob received all that he would ever receive by way of compensation: "Payment of the full amt.

claimed $36 is recommended." (Records of the Quartermaster General's Office, Miscellaneous Claims, Book G, #1775).

Hettie, along with her children and Tillie, remained at her parents' farm for four days after the conflict had ended. But the time finally came for Hettie to return to Gettysburg to find out what happened to her home, her neighbors and her town.

On the morning of July 7th Hettie, Sadie, Mollie and Tillie, wearing the same clothes in which they had left home a week before, began their journey back to town. What they saw along that three mile trek would be etched in their minds forever.

In one week, seven unforgettable days, their whole world was turned upside down. Taneytown Road was a mire of cavernous, mucky gullies burrowed out by the thousands of men, horses, caissons and wagons that used this road during the past week to get in and out of Gettysburg; despite its condition, it was still bustling with activity. In some places the road was impassable, so Hettie and the girls had to move to the fields in order to find firm ground to walk on.

As they trudged along they passed countless dead soldiers, horses and mules slaughtered during the bloodbath. More than 7,000 soldiers and 5,000 horses and mules were killed during the battle. Despite heroic efforts to remove and bury as many as possible, bodies of men and animals alike still lay on the ground or in shallow, hastily dug graves. Hugh Ziegler recalled that "[t]he dead were buried where they were left, in shallow graves, often with their feet sticking out . . ." (*Reminiscence of Hugh Ziegler of the Battle of Gettysburg.* Typescript, p. 4, from the Adams County Historical Society).

Most of the dead left on the fields at this point in time were Confederate soldiers. Since this area of the battlefield was by and large occupied by Union forces during the fighting, they would gather their dead for burial first, counting on others to come back to bury the Confederates.

The middle of July in south-central Pennsylvania is known for oppressive humidity, sweltering heat and temperatures that can reach well into the 90s. In the preceding week more than 12,000 dead bodies, both human and animal, had spent a considerable amount of time decaying in the hot summer sun. It was four days since the fighting ended, and hour by hour, still more were dying from their wounds.

As they headed toward the Evergreen Cemetery on the way back to their home on Baltimore Street, Hettie and her children would have seen what others described in their diaries.

> While passing along, the stench arising from the fields of carnage was most sickening. Dead horses, swollen to almost twice their natural size, lay in all directions, stains of blood frequently met our gaze, and all kinds of army accoutrements covered the ground. Fences had disappeared, some buildings were gone, others ruined. The whole landscape had been changed, and I felt as though we were in a strange and blighted land (Pierce, pp. 82-83).

> The dying and dead were all around us - men and beasts. We could count as high as twenty dead horses lying side by side. Imagine, if you can, the stench of one dead animal lying in the hot July sun for days. Here they were by the hundreds (Lydia Catherine Ziegler Clare. *A Gettysburg Girl's Story of the Great Battle*, © 1900. Typescript, Adams County Historical Society).

> We saw many terrible sights. Dead soldiers were lying around thick, dead horses, and many cow skins and heads . . . the many strange and terrible sights made a strong and lasting impression on my mind . . . . In one place there were as many as forty dead horses - where a battery had been planked; the bodies were much swollen . . . (McCreary, pp. 250-251).

Rudimentary sanitary conditions contributed the horror. There had been more than 165,000 soldiers in Gettysburg for the better part of a week; there were certainly not enough outhouses in the area to accommodate them. Add to that approximately 70,000 horses and mules doing their *business* as well. Sanitary conditions were inconceivably appalling. The stench was repulsive and nauseating!

> The atmosphere is loaded with the horrid smell of decaying horses and the remains of slaughtered animals, and, it is said, from the bodies of men imperfectly buried. I fear we shall be visited with pestilence, for every breath we draw is made ugly by the stench (Broadhead, p. 22).

For the next several months people rubbed strong-scented oils under their noses in an effort to seek relief from the odor, but to no avail. The carnage was so tremendous the stench would linger over the area throughout the summer and late into the fall. The repulsive odor was so intense it was said to have carried as far as Harrisburg, Pennsylvania, some thirty miles away. In the aftermath of the battle, Gettysburg was not only a very unpleasant place to be but a very unhealthy place as well.

> The stench from the battle-field after the fight was so bad that every one went about with a bottle of pennyroyal or peppermint oil. The burial of the dead commenced at once, and many were buried along the line where they fought and fell, and in many cases, so near the surface that their clothing came through the earth (McCreary, p. 251).

Continuing her journey home, Hettie once again took the shortcut through the Evergreen Cemetery. It was here only six days earlier, when passing the home of Peter and Elizabeth Thorn, caretakers for the cemetery, that soldiers had cautioned Hettie to find a safe place to hide. At that time soldiers were planting cannons and building stone breastworks in preparation for battle. Now the caretakers' home was hardly recognizable. Almost every window was shattered and the house was thoroughly ransacked; broken furniture and household items were scattered about the grounds.

They finally reached Baltimore Street, turned left toward town, and passed buildings riddled with bullet holes and streets covered with all manner of debris. They walked by and stepped over rifles, swords, canteens, belts, broken wagons, shattered caissons, ammunition, cartridge boxes, shoes and knapsacks. They saw fence posts standing where there had been board fences a week earlier. Kepis, bloody scraps of uniforms and body parts littered the streets as well. Because the wells were contaminated, there was no potable water, and there was barely a crumb of food left in town.

> The provisions we had in the house were soon consumed, and had it not been for the [Sanitary] Commission we should have starved to death. Their wagon stopped every morning with supplies of meat and bread and anything they had to distribute (McCreary, p. 250).

All along Baltimore Street an endless parade of people, soldiers and civilians alike, rushed here and there, each focused on some unpleasant task that needed to be done. The fighting had ended days earlier, and although there did not appear to be a sense of panic amidst the activity, there was still much confusion.

While Hettie was at her parents' farm outside of town, Union soldiers had shown great respect for the Weikert family and their home. They took what they needed (which, in the end, was just about everything the family had), but they did so in a firm, polite manner. Their courtesy was appreciated at the time, and since the Weikerts were loyal Unionists, no residual resentment was felt. Had their losses been at the hands of the Confederates, they would have obviously felt differently.

The citizens of Gettysburg had been petrified when the Rebels first occupied the streets of their town. They felt these invaders were coarse, smelly, rude men dressed in shabby uniforms who had not bathed for weeks or maybe months. For the most part Confederates, pursuant to Gen. Lee's Orders No. 72 and 73 (which forbade the seizure or injury of private property by his soldiers) did not unduly harass people who remained in their homes during the battle, but if a home were left unattended, that was a different story. Regardless of Lee's intention, more than a few houses were plundered, as Captain William Blackford witnessed firsthand during the time Confederates occupied a house along the "Main Street on the side next Cemetery Ridge." Blackford described the following scene:

> It was a strange sight to see these men fighting in these neatly and sometimes elegantly furnished rooms, while those not on duty reclined on elegant sofas, or stretched themselves out upon handsome carpets . . . feathers scattered everywhere in every room, upstairs and downstairs . . . done by shells bursting in feather beds . . . . Pools of blood in many places marked the spots where someone had been hit and laid out on the carpets, and here and there a dead body not yet removed . . . . On a marble table were set decanters of wine, around which were spread all sorts of delicacies taken from a sideboard in the adjoining dining room, where they had been left, in their hurry, by the inhabitants when they fled . . . (W. W. Blackford. *War Years With Jeb Stuart*. Scribners, 1945, pp. 231-232).

Sarah Broadhead witnessed the ransacking of a deserted home near her. She recalled:

> Part of the time we watched the Rebels rob the house opposite. The family had left some time during the day, and the robbers must have gotten all they left in the house. They went from the garret to the cellar, and loading up the plunder in a large four-horse wagon, drove it off (Broadhead, p. 13).

66

Albertus McCreary, who also lived on Baltimore Street, one block north of the Shrivers, witnessed Confederate destruction as well:

> There were some sorry-looking homes in our neighborhood. The Confederate soldiers had entered them during their occupation of the town and tried to see how much damage they could do . . . almost everything had either been cut to pieces or destroyed in some way. Pieces of furniture were burned and broken, a desk had been destroyed, bookcases knocked down, and the books torn and shattered. To add more to the disorder and destruction, the soldiers had taken a half-barrel of flour, mixed it with water to make a thin paste, put into this the feathers from feather-beds and thrown it over everything - walls, furniture and down the stairways (McCreary, p. 250).

Charles Tyson, a photographer who lived just east of the Diamond recounted what he discovered when he returned home:

> My secretary [desk] was ransacked and the contents scattered over the room. In the parlor we found a small heap of ashes, the residue of burned letters and papers . . . . All my clothing was taken and several Rebel suits left in place . . . [The Confederates had] emptied a barrel of ninety-five percent alcohol. I had a gross of eight ounce bottles there also and they were seen carrying these bottles out filled with alcohol (Typescript. Adams County Historical Society, pp. 2-3).

Upon returning to her apartment at the Lutheran Seminary, Lydia Catherine Ziegler Clare wrote, "Oh, what a home-coming! Everything we owned was gone - not a bed to lie on, and not a change of clothing. Many things had been destroyed, and the rest had been converted to hospital purposes" (Clare *op. cit.*).

As Hettie made her way up Baltimore Street, she undoubtedly discovered most of her household possessions strewn about in front of her home. During the battle Confederates had set up a barricade across Baltimore Street in the general area where that road connects with Breckinridge Street; this enabled more of their soldiers to shoot southward toward Union forces on Cemetery Hill. The barricade was constructed of any readily available materials such as furniture, sofas, mattresses, benches, crates, tables, barrels, etc. Since the Shrivers' home had been deserted during the battle, there would have been no one to stop the Confederates from helping themselves to whatever they needed. For this reason, the Shrivers' home would have been in shambles when Hettie returned. In addition to the items they needed to build the barricade, soldiers would have helped themselves to any food found in the Shrivers' two kitchens, unripened fruits and vegetables in the garden (since it was early in the growing season), supplies, clothing, blankets, linens, curtains, tools and any *booty* they spied such as money, silver or liquor. One can only imagine what Hettie found when she entered the once beautiful home she and George had built just three short years earlier.

When Hettie dropped Tillie off at her home, the Pierces hardly recognized their daughter because she was still wearing the same clothes she had worn when she left with Hettie - and she had not bathed for more than a week. Hettie learned from Tillie's parents that, just as she and her family had done at the Weikert farm, most folks in town also hid in their cellars during the fighting.

The thought of hiding in one's cellar in the midst of a horrific battle and not knowing what was going on outside had to be terrifying. Folks who squeezed into a confined, dark and, in some cases, wet space with no way to shut out the sounds of conflict, could only imagine what was going on around them - and, perhaps, that was even worse than actually knowing.

The time that we sat in the cellar seemed long, listening to the terrific sound of the strife; more terrible never greeted human ears. We knew that with every explosion, and the scream of each shell, human beings were being hurried, through excruciating pain, into another world, and that many more were torn, and mangled, and lying in torment worse than death, and no one able to extend relief. The thought made me very sad . . . . Some thought this awful afternoon would never come to a close (Broadhead, p. 15).

Catherine Garlach, Hettie's neighbor to the south, also remained in her home during the battle, spending much of that time hiding in the cellar with her children and a few neighbors. Catherine's daughter, Anna Kitzmiller (nee Garlach), later remembered events this way:

I was a girl of about 18 at the time of the battle and our family was composed of my father, mother, my brother Will, 12 years old at that time, Sister Katie, and Frank the baby of 6 months and myself . . . .

The morning of the battle my father . . . went to the Cemetery Hill to watch the fighting that could be seen from that point. When he attempted to come home he was stopped by soldiers and told that he was a spy and that he could not go into town. He went back down the country and did not get back until July 5th or 6th . . . (Interview. *Gettysburg Compiler*. August 23, 1905).

On that first day of battle, July 1, about the time Hettie finally reached the Weikert farmhouse, Confederate forces had overrun the town compelling Union troops to retreat down Baltimore Street toward Cemetery Hill. Anna Kitzmiller continued describing these harrowing events:

In the retreat on the first day there were more people in the street than I have seen since at any time. The street seemed blocked. In front of our house the crowd was so great that I believe I could have walked across the street on the heads of the soldiers . . . . The soldiers in retreat called to us, 'Go to the cellar, go to the cellar.'

Since much of Gettysburg sits over a very high water table, many cellars in town are prone to flooding during heavy rains. Because the last week of June, 1863, was one of those rainy periods, the Garlach's cellar was flooded at the time of the battle. Their cellar, as in most homes at the time, consisted of a hard-packed, dirt floor with a ceiling little more than five feet high. Added to the obvious concerns related to the conflict raging around them was the fact that her husband, Henry, had not yet returned from his wanderings about the battlefield. Generally wet and miserable in her cramped quarters, Mrs. Garlach made the decision to leave her house and take her family next door. This move was described by Anna Kitzmiller:

> Our cellar had a foot or more of water in it and after we had been told several times to go to the cellar mother took us to the next house up the street [the Shrivers'] where there was a ten pin alley and we went into [the] basement of the house and we were hardly there before the Rebels appeared over Baltimore hill and out Breckenridge street and began firing (*Gettysburg Compiler*, August 23, 1905).

From the cellar windows of the Shrivers' home overlooking Baltimore Street, the sills of which sit at street level, the Garlach family had a clear view of the action on the street and the furor that took place just a few feet in front of them, as the Confederates prepared to stop any advance of Union troops from Cemetery Hill. They could hear the non-stop gunfire and men shouting orders on the smoke-filled street, even watch as men and horses were killed before their eyes. Anna Kitzmiller recalled seeing "a cannon at Pierce's corner for a short time."

The Garlachs may have occupied the cellar, but the rest of the Shrivers' home belonged to the Confederates. Each group was well aware of the other, but both stayed out of each other's way. Here is how Anna remembered what happened next (again, in her interview of August 23, 1905):

> After dark we went back to our own home and mother made beds on the floor and we slept there. She was afraid if we occupied the beds bullets would come in the windows and reach us . . . .
>
> It was a great strain on mother to be left alone for she did not know what had become of father . . . . Neighbors drifted into our house until by evening of the first day there were 15 souls in our home, 11 besides our own family. . . .

During the second day of the fighting, rather than chance being out in the open to make yet another dash to the Shrivers' cellar, Catherine Garlach and her son gathered scraps of wood from her husband's cabinet-making shop to erect platforms in their cellar to enable them to sit above the water.

While the Garlachs were hiding, first in the Shrivers' cellar and then in their own, Mr. Pierce and his family were hiding in their cellar. However, even with the fury surrounding his family, Mr. Pierce was curious about what was happening outside during the battle, so he made frequent trips to his garret to peer out the windows. The Pierce home had one small north-facing window and two large south-facing windows providing him a spectacular view of much of the southern end of town, particularly Cemetery Hill. When Mr. Pierce looked through his south-facing windows he could easily see into the Shrivers' garret window and was presented with a close-up view of an amazing scene. He later reported he saw "a number of rebel sharpshooters, busy at their work of picking off our men" (Pierce, p. 94).

Mr. Pierce had a birds-eye view of a Rebel sharpshooters nest inside the Shrivers' garret just a few yards from his window. Mr. Pierce observed soldiers removing bricks on either side of the Shrivers' south-facing window in order to create two small loopholes (what he referred to as *port holes*) through which they could fire on their Union adversaries on Cemetery Hill. Each time a Confederate sharpshooter fired his rifle through one of the loopholes, a cloud of grey smoke would drift out the end of the barrel, thus revealing his presence to Union Sharpshooters who would fire back. Firing through these loopholes, rather than through the larger garret window, Confederates would be less exposed to return Union fire.

Shrivers' Garret

A constant parade of soldiers climbed into the Shrivers' garret carrying supplies, boxes of ammunition and buckets of water, since it was dreadfully hot in this crowded and confined space. Mr. Pierce watched as a Confederate soldier, after firing his rifle through one of the loopholes, suddenly threw his arms up into the air and crashed down onto the floor. There was an immediate atmosphere of confusion, and a short time later several men carried the dead soldier from the garret, down the stairs and outside through Hettie's garden.

In a letter dated July 19, 1863, Hettie's neighbor, John Rupp, whose tannery Hettie had passed on her way to and from the Weikert farm, wrote to his sister in Baltimore that Union troops "killed two up in Mr. G. Schriver's garret." (Letter, Adams County Historical Society).

Anna Kitzmiller also described seeing sharpshooters "in the [Shrivers'] house . . . just north of our home. They had taken out a row of brick on the second floor from which they fired towards Cemetery Hill. As every point occupied by sharp-shooters became a special target our house was repeatedly hit."

∿∿ ∿∿ ∿∿

With more than 20,000 severely wounded soldiers left behind after the fighting, virtually every public building and many houses in the area served as hospitals. Some homes were overflowing with injured soldiers; in other homes, families cared for only one or, perhaps, several wounded men.

> Can we endure the spectacle of hundreds of men wounded in every conceivable manner, some in the head and limbs, here an arm off and there a leg, and just inside a poor fellow with both legs shot away? It is dreadful to behold. . . . Nearly every house is a hospital, besides the churches and the warehouses, and there are many field hospitals scattered over the country near the scene of the battle (Broadhead, pp. 17-20).

> For months after the battle, Gettysburg and the surrounding country for miles was one vast hospital. Every church, the College and Seminary buildings, in fact every public building, and many houses and barns were used for hospital purposes, and a general hospital was established in and near the grove on the hill to the east of Gettysburg (Gettysburg Compiler, July 3, 1912).

There were a number of hospitals within a block of us . . . and many private residences near by were all turned to the same account. We were saved much annoyance by having a red flag put up at our door to show that the house was a hospital (McCreary, pp. 249-250).

During the fighting a red flag indicated a place where wounded soldiers could seek immediate care and treatment. Afterwards, it designated a place where soldiers could find food, water, bandages, other supplies and medical assistance. Even later, it indicated a place where wounded loved ones might be found by anxious relatives in search of them. A wide variety of flags made of everything from old shirts, scarves or just small scraps of red fabric, flew around town. The flag was tacked or tied to a stick, although occasionally, it was simply nailed to the front of the house. When Hettie returned she would have seen such a red flag over her front door as well.

The Shrivers' large, four-bedroom house, which included two kitchens and a 14' x 65', two-lane, fully enclosed ten-pin alley, was sitting empty since the Confederates departed. It offered plenty of space to aid in the care of the wounded. With so many other private residences serving as hospitals, the Shrivers' home, undoubtedly, served in this capacity as well.

Almost as soon as the fighting ended, thousands of people from all around the country began pouring into town. Some came to comfort wounded loved ones, others to retrieve their dead, and still others, out of curiosity, to see the site of the glorious victory they read about in newspaper accounts.

Our town was filled up every day by people coming from all over the country - fathers, mothers, brothers, sisters hunting their wounded or dead and the scenes on the streets near the improvised hospitals where the relatives were having their loved ones prepared for shipment by the large number of undertakers who had come into Gettysburg for the purpose, were indeed distressing (Skelly, p. 26).

> The town is as full as ever of strangers, and the old story of the inability of a village of twenty-five hundred inhabitants, overrun and eaten out by two large armies, to accommodate from ten to twelve thousand visitors, is repeated almost hourly (Broadhead, p. 23).

While the monumental task of cleaning up after the battle commenced, the citizens of Gettysburg tried their best to return to some sense of normalcy. Houses were cleaned and furnishings were repaired or replaced. Gardens and farmlands were replanted with crops that, given the short amount of growing time left in the year, might yet produce some provisions for the long winter to come. In addition to restoring order in her home, Hettie's walls and floors were scrubbed to remove bloodstains and any indication of the men wounded, killed and cared for there. Bricks were replaced in the two gaping loopholes that had been knocked through the side of the garret wall.

> The months following the conflict found many extra burdens placed on the town, but there was a willing response on the part of its citizens on all occasions and the confusion that might be expected as an aftermath of such a staggering calamity was reduced to a minimum (Skelly, p. 25).

Eventually, as the wounded were treated and released, transferred to larger hospitals or hospitals in their home towns, or in a great many cases, died of their wounds, fewer hospitals were needed. Ultimately all the remaining wounded were consolidated into one large hospital, named *Camp Letterman*, about a mile east of the Diamond on the road to York.

The next several months were busy ones in Gettysburg as the chaotic summer finally came to a close. On numerous occasions during the fall, Hettie Shriver's name appeared in *The Adams Sentinel* under the *List of Letters* remaining in the Post Office. Since mail was not delivered to one's door at the time, the newspaper published the names of those who had received correspondence or parcels so that these could be picked up from the Postmaster. We can only wonder if any of these were letters from George.

Interring the dead in a dignified and orderly manner became a high priority for the residents of Gettysburg. Plans were made for the creation of a national cemetery to specifically honor the Union soldiers who fought and gave their lives here. In November, a little over four months after the battle ended, thousands of people came to witness the dedication of this new cemetery. Gettysburg was once again inundated with hordes of visitors. Some were folks who had lost loved ones on this and countless other battlefields during the war, and, once again, some were just curious onlookers.

Edward Everett, one of the nation's great orators at that time, was invited to deliver the principal speech at the dedication of the Soldiers' National Cemetery. At the last minute, and purely as a courtesy, an invitation was also extended to President Abraham Lincoln who, to the surprise of many, accepted.

> Our town was filled with people who had come in during the several previous days for the dedication of the cemetery. We had but four ordinary-sized hotels of a capacity such as a town of 2,300 people would require for the entertainment of visitors during ordinary occasions. These were filled to overflowing and all private houses were also filled to capacity by friends of the families and as many other visitors as could be accommodated. I was up until after midnight on November 18th and there were many people walking the streets, unable to get any accommodations for the night (Skelly, p. 26).

President Lincoln arrived at Gettysburg around 5:00 p.m. after a long ride from Washington, D.C., and stayed at the home of Attorney David Wills on the southeast corner of the Diamond. The next morning, November 19th, around 10:00 a.m., President Lincoln rode horseback down Baltimore Street. Long legs dangling

President Lincoln's procession down Baltimore Street
passed directly in front of the Shrivers' home (outlined).

and coat tails flopping, Lincoln rode past the Shrivers' home on
route to the site of the dedication. Because a visit to Gettysburg by
the President of the United States was truly a momentous occasion,
Hettie and her children would not only have witnessed Lincoln's
procession past their home, they would have also heard his
immortal words. Since she did not write of the experience, however,
we must turn to someone who did:

> I recall very vividly my impressions of Mr.
> Lincoln as I walked close to him . . . . His face, lined
> and sad, bore traces of the tremendous worry the
> ordeal of war had brought to him. His expression
> was benign and kindly, and the strength of his
> character seemed to me to be evidenced in the
> pronounced features, a high forehead, a prominent
> nose and a decided chin jutting below firmly-set lips.
> His countenance seemed to reflect the tragedy of war

and the significance of his visit to Gettysburg on that day (Skelly, p. 27).

The procession arrived at the cemetery and, as was customary for speakers at the time, Mr. Everett, the primary speaker, spoke for more than two hours. President Lincoln spoke next and, in sharp contrast to Mr. Everett's lengthy oration, his speech lasted less than three minutes. His immortal words, though, would never be forgotten. Abraham Lincoln's carefully crafted address came to be regarded as one of the greatest speeches in American history. After the dedication of the cemetery, President Lincoln spent several more hours in Gettysburg before boarding the train back to Washington, D.C.

The horrendous stench of death that permeated the town since the beginning of July was finally dissipating as the first cold winds of winter swept over Adams County. Christmas was only a few weeks away, and Hettie could only hope and pray that George would get home to see Mollie and Sadie during the upcoming holidays. Sadie had been five years old when George left her and the family to go to war, and she would surely yearn to have her father with them at Christmas. Mollie, on the other hand, had been a mere four year old child at the time. Would she even remember her father?

~~~ ~~~ ~~~

George Shriver enlisted in the Union Army on August 27, 1861, for a term of three years. He was mustered into service on September 9th in Frederick, Maryland, approximately 30 miles south of Gettysburg. As a 5th Corporal in Co. C., Cole's Cavalry, Maryland Volunteers, 1st Potomac Home Brigade, he served under the command of Capt. John Horner. Cole's Cavalry was an elite group of soldiers that earned a fine reputation.

They were . . . intelligent, enthusiastic, accustomed to the use of firearms, of fine physique - in fact, the very best material for cavalrymen.

Their thorough knowledge of the topography of the country, which became, to a great extent, the seat of the war in West Maryland, Pennsylvania and Virginia, rendered their services to the Union cause invaluable. During the four long years of war from 1861 to 1865, they were almost constantly in the saddle, and from Gettysburg, in Pennsylvania, to Lynchburg, on the James, in Virginia, they scouted and fought with untiring zeal (L. Allison Wilmer, J.H. Jarrett, and George W.F. Vernon. "Cole's Cavalry, First Regiment Potomac Home Brigade Cavalry," in *Maryland Volunteers, War of 1861-5.* Baltimore: Guggenheimer, Weil & Co., 1898, vol. 1, pp. 655-656).

The *U.S. Regimental Descriptive Book* described George as 5'9" tall with a light complexion, dark eyes and light hair. His occupation was listed as *Inn Keeper*. George was issued the following items: a carbine (#32328), pistol (#35675), saber, saddle, bridle, halter, nose bag, curry comb and brush, horse blanket and spurs (Adams County Historical Society).

Before entering into battle the men of Cole's Cavalry attended training camp in Frederick, Maryland, where they would undergo instructions in drilling and learning the duties of a soldier. Over the next two years Co. C of Cole's Cavalry was engaged in countless skirmishes and battles throughout Maryland and Virginia in places like Hancock, Winchester, Cedar Creek, Strausburg, Harper's Ferry, Sharpsburg, Fountain Dale, Snickersville, Leesburg, Rector's Cross Roads, Charlestown, Mount Jackson, Woodstock, Ashby's Gap, Front Royal, Edinburg, New Market, Harrisonburg, Romney, Moorefield and more.

Albert M. Hunter, another member of Co. C., Cole's Cavalry, was also George's cousin. He entered the service as a bugler and rose to the rank of Captain, replacing Capt. Horner, and served during the entire war before mustering out four years later. In a letter to his niece, Albert wrote the following:

I was sent out on picket, just at sun down our pickets were fired on by a squad of Rebels. They fired and came into the reserve double quick. John Dullar who always boasted of how he could fight a hundred [Confederates], jumped on his horse and started back. Geo. Shriver saw him first and called 'come back you cowardly rascal' but he rode on . . . . Shriver was a quiet man and no one thought he was much of the soldier, but the occurrence recorded above and is [sic] another proof to allow talks don't make the best soldier (Letter. Emmitsburg Historical Society).

On February 26, 1863, Cole's Cavalry *Morning Reports* attests that George Shriver *Returned from Hospital*. No reason was given for why he was admitted or how long he was there.

Cole's Cavalry did not always travel as one unit. On many occasions small bands of soldiers were detached to scout the countryside or placed on special duty. During the Battle of Gettysburg, records indicate the men of Co. C were stationed in various locations between Gettysburg, Pennsylvania and Frederick, Maryland. Since specific information regarding the placement of each individual soldier is not available, it is not known if George was in Gettysburg during the battle or if he served elsewhere.

In December, 1863, just a little over five months after the battle ravaged his home town, George was granted a four-day furlough. This meant he could spend Christmas with his family.

George had been away for more than two years, camped out in all manner of weather and conditions, spent thousands of hours on horseback, and did not eat or bathe regularly. When he arrived home on December 26th, George would have appeared haggard and much older than his 27 years; he would have looked much different than the man who had left home only a few years before. One can scarcely imagine not only the joy of every member of this family to have George home, but of his surprise at seeing how much Sadie and Mollie had grown since he had last seen them. George was finally home, and they could celebrate Christmas as a family. For the Shrivers there could be no better Christmas gift.

After spending a few precious days at home with his family, however, George's furlough was over and it was time for him to report back to duty. As difficult as it had been to say farewell back in September, 1861, when George initially left to join the military, the pain of that separation could not compare to the heartbreak in saying goodbye this time. George had endured much over the past two years, and his family had had incredible experiences themselves, particularly over the preceding several months. War no longer seemed quite so noble, romantic or glorious now that each of them had personally seen and experienced the horrors of battle. How distressing it must have been for George and Hettie knowing how much more the girls would understand this time.

George returned to duty on December 29th, 1863, near Brandy Station, Virginia. Three days later, January 1, 1864, Cole's Cavalry was engaged in off-and-on fighting with the 43rd Battalion of Virginia Cavalry, an elite guerrilla unit led by John S. Mosby and more popularly known - and dreaded - as Mosby's Rangers. Some eighty members of Cole's Cavalry, commanded by George's cousin, Capt. Albert N. Hunter, were proceeding toward Rectortown, Virginia, when they encountered Mosby's men. During the skirmish that ensued, Hunter's horse was shot out from under him, and his men fled toward nearby Middleburg, Virginia. In the melee, Confederates killed, wounded or captured fifty-seven Union soldiers (Jeffrey D. Wert. *Mosby's Rangers*, Simon and Schuster, 1990, pp. 131-132).

The January 11, 1864, edition of the *Gettysburg Compiler* reported an account of the engagement listing the names of the casualties. Under the list of those *taken prisoners and missing* appeared the name *Corporal George W. Shriver.*

Two weeks later, January 14, 1864, despite the fact that he was a prisoner of war, George was promoted from Corporal to Sergeant.

ᨆ ᨆ ᨆ

In November of 1863, a small village in southern Georgia had been selected as a site to build a desperately needed Confederate prison for captured Union soldiers. The Deep South location, availability of fresh water, and its proximity to the Southwestern Railroad, made this a favorable location for a prison. Construction of a 16½ acre camp to house approximately 10,000 Union prisoners of war was begun in January, 1864. By late February the first prisoners arrived at Camp Sumter, more commonly known as Andersonville. The exact date of George Shriver's arrival at Andersonville Prison is not known, but the historic record affirms he was there. Another member of Co. C., Cole's Cavalry, Theodore McAlister, a resident of Gettysburg and a fellow captive at Andersonville, later had this to say about George Shriver:

> . . . the men of this prison were very rarely given anything to eat. What little they did receive was chopped corn and cobs mixed together. As George was always accustomed to a good living on his father's farm, he soon became very sick (*History of the Shriver Family.* Privately printed, n.d.).

George was admitted to the Andersonville prison hospital on March 22nd suffering from catarrh (an inflammation of the mucus membranes, especially the nose and throat). He returned to the prison on March 30th.

Less than two weeks later, on April 10th, George was back in the prison hospital, this time suffering from diarrhea. He remained in the hospital for more than two weeks, returning to the camp on April 27th.

By early June the population of the camp had climbed to 20,000. The prison was so overcrowded the camp walls were expanded to add an additional ten acres. Life in Andersonville was a living nightmare. There was no shelter from the sun or rain and disease ran rampant throughout the overcrowded camp. There was very little food; water was supplied from the same stream used as a latrine; and every possession, no matter how small, was a treasure to be protected with one's life. What began as isolated incidents of prisoners preying upon other prisoners for their meager possessions became an epidemic when a number of prisoners formed gangs to terrorize the camp. The most infamous of these gangs, known as *Mosby's Raiders*, stole food, money, clothing and property by brute force. Prison authorities did nothing to stop their relentless domination of the other inmates, and prisoners who fought back were subject to severe gang beatings. In July of 1864, however, a group of prisoners calling themselves the *Regulators* banded together to oppose the Raiders. Captain Henry Wirz, Commandant of Camp Sumter, gave permission to the prison population to put the Raiders on trial and promised to carry out their verdicts. The Raiders were rounded up and found guilty by a jury of newly-arrived prisoners, fresh off the train and unfamiliar with their exploits. Six men, who were identified as ring-leaders of the gang, were hanged inside the prison stockade on July 11, 1864. Such was the brutality George had to witness and endure on a daily basis.

By August over 30,000 Union prisoners were being held in the 26½ acre site; the death rate was climbing to nearly 100 per day.

On August 25, 1864, after more than six months in captivity in Andersonville, George Shriver died of scurvy and starvation; he was 28 years old. Once a man died his fellow inmates would strip the body, tie a tag to his toe indicating his name and military unit, and place the body by the stockade gate to be removed and buried.

Andersonville Prison held 32,899 prisoners at its most crowded. During its fifteen months of operation, almost 13,000 Union prisoners died there of malnutrition, exposure and disease. Over 40% of all Union prisoners of war who died during the Civil War perished at Andersonville.

Hettie had last seen George on December 29, 1863. George was taken prisoner only three days later, but almost two weeks would go by before his capture was reported in the *Gettysburg Compiler* on January 11, 1864. Many agonizing months would pass without Hettie knowing the fate of her husband, beyond the fact that he was a prisoner. She would do her best to be strong for Sadie and Mollie, but one can only imagine the lonely nights Hettie spent lying awake in her bed wondering *when* George would be coming home, indeed, *if* he would ever be coming home.

It was almost a year from the time George had said his final good-byes to Hettie, Sadie and Mollie following their Christmas visit that Hettie learned of George's death. On December 12, 1864, the *Gettysburg Compiler* reported: "George Shriver, who was taken prisoner . . . died whilst in the hands of the rebels."

~~~ ~~~ ~~~

In 1865, President Abraham Lincoln appointed Clara Barton, a nurse and humanitarian from Massachusetts, to search for the missing men of the Union army. Her work resulted in tracing the fate of approximately 30,000 men. When the war ended she was sent to Andersonville, Georgia, to set up and mark the graves of the Union soldiers buried there. As a result of Barton's commitment, 12,000 graves were officially marked, and Andersonville became a national cemetery on August 17, 1865. Barton, who raised the U.S. flag the day the cemetery was dedicated, was overcome by emotion and later wrote in her diary:

> Up and there it drooped as if in grief and sadness, till at length the sunlight streamed out and its beautiful folds filled - the men struck up the Star Spangled Banner, and I covered my face and wept (Clara Barton. *Diary*, August 17, 1865).

George Shriver is buried in grave #6816
in Andersonville National Cemetery.

Coming from well-to-do families and owing to the sale of his father's farm, George and Hettie had been fortunate to have the economic resources, at quite a young age, to buy property, build their new home and start a new business venture. Five years later, however, with no income except George's meager military pay, Hettie's financial position would have been seriously strained.

Upon George's death Hettie was entitled to file a claim against his military pension. Part of the filing process required witnesses to attest to her relationship to George. On June 3, 1865, two of Hettie's Baltimore Street neighbors, Henry Garlach and Jacob Benner, testified:

> . . . that they have been for five years well acquainted with Henrietta Schriver and George W. Schriver . . . having removed to Gettysburg aforesaid about five years ago to the property where the said Henrietta Schriver, widow of the said George W. Schriver deceased soldier, now lives excepting the first year when they lived on the other side of the street (From a copy reproduced at the National Archives).

Before he left home to join the cavalry, George had completed construction of both the saloon and ten-pin alley, but his business never opened because he never returned from the war. A widow at twenty-nine, Hettie now had to fend for herself and her two daughters, but running the saloon was not an option available to her. For a woman to do so would have been unimaginable in the mid-19th century. With very little money left and no husband to support her, Hettie, according to the conventions of the time, was left with very few options. She would have to sell their beautiful home and she would have to remarry.

On March 30, 1866, Hettie was forced to face the reality of her new life without George when she sold her home on Baltimore Street. The Shrivers had originally purchased a lot-and-a-half of property. Hettie sold the house and half of the side lot to Daniel

Trimmer for $2,100, but she hold onto the half-lot (30') closest to the Garlach's property. Daniel Trimmer and Hettie's neighbor, Henry Garlach, were partners in the cabinet-making business advertised as *Garlach & Trimmer*.

On July 19, 1866, a year and a half after receiving word of George's death and three months after selling her home, Hettie

Daniel Free Pittenturf

married a widower, Daniel Free (sometimes spelled "Ferree") Pittenturf. Daniel, who was born in Heidlersburg, Pennsylvania (about ten miles northeast of Gettysburg), made his living as a stone-mason and a blacksmith. Daniel worked for, and lived next door to, his first wife's parents, Solomon and Catherine Powers, on West High Street.

Hettie and her girls moved from their large, finely-appointed, 36' wide home to Daniel's modest, 14' wide house which Sadie and Mollie would share

with two step-brothers. The move was only a block away; but it was worlds apart from the comfortable lifestyle they had always known.

Daniel's first wife, Cynthia, the oldest of six Powers sisters, died on April 25, 1864. When the fighting in Gettysburg ended, the Powers family had taken a number of wounded soldiers into their home located at the corner of Washington and High Streets. Cynthia and her sisters spent countless hours nursing wounded men in the dank cellar of their parents' home causing Cynthia, who had delivered a baby just six months earlier, to become quite ill. Cynthia died nine months later, leaving Daniel with two young sons, Frank Powers (age 2) and James Powers (age 1).

It is impossible to know if Hettie married Daniel out of love or convenience. She was a widow with two young daughters to care for while he was a widower raising two sons alone. Hettie needed someone to support her and her daughters; Daniel needed a mother for his sons. They married long before the lengthy mourning period a widow would have traditionally observed. More than 600,000 soldiers died during the four years of the Civil War leaving thousands of widows behind. Under the circumstances, general society observed a period of leniency which permitted women to marry well short of the conventional period of mourning.

Less than three months after Hettie and Daniel were wed, James was killed in a bizarre accident. On October 9, 1866, *The Adams Sentinel* reported:

> Mournful Event. A little son [James] of Mr. Daniel F. Pittenturf, and a grand-child of Mr. Solomon Powers, of this place, aged about 3 years, fell into a bucket of scalding water which was near the door of the kitchen, on Saturday last, and was so much injured as to cause his death the next morning.

After James' death, Daniel's in-laws, Solomon and Catherine Powers, petitioned the court and were subsequently awarded custody of their grandson, Frank Powers (called *Powers* by the family), forcing Daniel to give up the rights to his only surviving son.

Hettie and Daniel were married less than a year when, on April 17, 1867, Hettie gave birth to their first child and Daniel's first daughter, Lillie Mae. A little over two years later another daughter, whom they named Emma, arrived on September 12, 1869. Unfortunately, she lived less than a month. Emma died on October 11th of *Cholera Infantum* (an often fatal form of gastroenteritis occurring in infants, not of the same cause as cholera but having somewhat similar characteristics) and was laid to rest in the Evergreen Cemetery.

According to the 1870 U.S. Census records, Daniel and Henrietta Pittenturf were listed immediately before Solomon and Catherine Powers who still lived on High Street in Gettysburg. Daniel's surviving son, Powers, however, is listed as residing with his grandparents, Solomon and Catherine Powers. Therefore, although

Powers was raised by his grandparents, he lived in the house next door to his father, Daniel.

On November 6, 1874, just two weeks shy of her nineteenth birthday, Sadie Shriver died. Her death certificate lists the cause as *consumption*, what is known today as tuberculosis. She was buried in the Evergreen Cemetery.

On December 1, 1878, Mollie married William E. Stallsmith, a young man from nearby Littlestown. But tragedy would strike once again. When the 1880 census was taken on June 1st, William and Mollie were residing in Gettysburg on Baltimore Street - the same street Mollie had lived on as a child. William's occupation was recorded as carpenter; Mollie's occupation was listed as housewife, but it was also noted she was suffering from dyspepsia (difficulty digesting food). Six weeks later, on July 16, 1880, less than a month before her twenty-third birthday, Mollie, too, died of consumption. Married for less than two years, Mollie was buried in the Stallsmith family plot in Evergreen Cemetery.

Lillie, Hettie's only surviving daughter, married William Allen Hollebaugh on July 12, 1885. By 1890, William Allen, as he was called by the family, and Lillie moved to Harrisburg, Pennsylvania. Within a year, Hettie and Daniel moved in with their daughter and son-in-law, where the two men manufactured and sold cigars.

Hettie, Daniel, Lillie and William Allen then moved to Baltimore, Maryland, in the late 1890s. While living there, Daniel died on March 17, 1900, at the age of 71.

When the 1900 census was taken, records confirm Hettie was living on N. Washington Street in Baltimore, Maryland, with Lillie and her husband, William Allen, and their four children: Henrietta Pearl (known simply as *Pearl*) who was 13 years old at the time; Ruby L., seven years old; and William Allen, Jr., called *Billy*, four years old.

In time, however, Lillie and William Allen moved their family to Washington, D.C., but Hettie did not make the move with them. She moved to Annapolis to live with her granddaughter, Pearl, and her family.

When the 1910 Census was taken, records indicate Hettie was still living in Annapolis with her granddaughter, Pearl, Pearl's husband, Samuel Reese Abbott, and their four year old daughter, Ruth Lillian.

Hettie's granddaughter, Pearl,
with her daughter, Ruth.

A few years later, Hettie, once again, moved in with her daughter, Lillie, who was still residing in Washington, D.C.

Henrietta Weikert Shriver Pittenturf died of *acute gastritis, senility* in her daughter's home on April 7, 1916, and is buried with her daughter, Lillie, in Glenwood Cemetery in Washington, D.C.

Hettie was married to George for less than ten years and they were separated by war for close to three of those ten years. Of their three children Jacob died at birth, while Sadie and Mollie both died before bearing children of their own. Although there are still quite a few Shrivers living in the Gettysburg area today, none are descendants of George and Hettie Shriver.

Hettie and Daniel were married for more than thirty-three years. Of their two children, Emma lived less than a month, leaving Lillie to be the only one of Hettie's five children to survive to adulthood.

The Battle of Gettysburg resulted in more than 51,000 military casualties and has been chronicled from almost every point of view. Although millions of people still read about and visit Gettysburg as an important battlefield of the Civil War, the history of what happened on that battlefield is more than just the story of large-scale troop movements and military maneuvers. It is the story of individuals who left their families to serve their country, soldiers like George Shriver. It is also the story of the families they left behind, civilians like Hettie, Sadie and Mollie Shriver. Their lives - soldiers and civilians alike - were forever changed as a result of the events that occurred on the picturesque rolling hills of Gettysburg, Pennsylvania, in 1863.

Restoration of the Shriver House

In 1983 my husband, Del Gudmestad, and I were working in the computer industry in my hometown of Philadelphia. Disillusioned by the corporate world, we wanted to work for ourselves, so after exploring a wide variety of options, we finally settled on opening a bed and breakfast. After considering a number of locations, we determined Gettysburg best fit our dreams and our business plan. We were married less than a year when we moved to Gettysburg on July 4, 1984, and opened up the first bed and breakfast in town, the Old Appleford Inn. As the majority of our guests came to tour the battlefield, lively discussions about practically every imaginable aspect of the battle took place around the breakfast table each morning. Neither my husband nor I were Civil War enthusiasts, but it did not take us long to realize the one topic never brought up in these exchanges was what happened to the 2,400 people living in Gettysburg in 1863 who suddenly found themselves in the midst of the most famous battle in American history. It became clear to us that visitors who came to learn about the Battle of Gettysburg also needed to know the other side of the story.

We started to compile stories of local families and their experiences during the conflict; since some of the fiercest fighting in town took place on Baltimore Street that seemed to be the perfect location for telling these stories. Over the course of several years, we looked at numerous houses as they became available for sale on the southern end of Baltimore Street, near Cemetery Hill. We sought to acquire a building which could be used as a backdrop for telling the effects of the battle on the civilians living in Gettysburg at the time and to give visitors an opportunity to tour an authentic Civil War house enabling them to see what see what home-life was like in the mid-19th century.

We were not having much success until we inquired about a neglected, desolate-looking, brick house sitting about halfway between Lincoln Square in the center of town and the Visitor Center at the Gettysburg National Military Park. The owner of the property had no interest in selling, but after calling on him more times than I care to admit, we finally persuaded him to sell. Our first walk through the house was quite an experience! It was obvious the house, which had been painted green, was divided in half at some point; one of the windows on the first floor had been converted into a door in order to provide a second entrance from the street. The southern half of the house was occupied and habitable, but definitely needed work. The northern half, however, had been abandoned for nearly thirty years! It had missing window panes, no electricity, no water, no heat and a serious leak in the roof. At one time, we learned, nearly thirty cats lived in the abandoned half of the house. But, in our eyes, this uninviting fixer-upper was perfect. Anyone who loves old homes knows, however, the only thing to be counted on during any restoration is that it will take twice as long and cost twice as much as originally calculated.

While the house was undergoing a major restoration, we continued to research the stories of civilians living in town during the battle. In addition to sharing the stories of other families, we obviously wanted to find out everything we could about our newly acquired property: Who built the house? What was the owner's occupation? And what happened to the residents of the house during the battle? It was difficult to find anyone who could give us much information about the house or its original owners, but after countless hours of arduous research, George and Hettie Shriver's story gradually began to unfold.

It was a mere chance of fate to find a house which had been altered very little since it was originally built just a few months before the Civil War began. Two major changes, although drastic, fortunately had not affected that portion of the house originally occupied by the Shriver family. Sometime in the late 1800s the ten-pin alley in the back yard was torn down. In the early 1900s the

The Shriver's home sat abandoned for nearly
30 years before the restoration in 1996.

house was divided into two rental properties, and two separate additions were added to the rear of the house, one for each half. Although this was an unfortunate alteration it presented one small bit of luck. Since these two additions were built to accommodate indoor plumbing for each side of the divided house, modern kitchens and bathrooms were never placed within the original Shrivers' home. Except that one window in each of the rear rooms of the original house had been modified to provide doorways to the rear additions, the house still appeared much the way it did in 1863.

In the mid-19th century, most household items were included in the sale of a home, but when Hettie sold her home, however, she elected to exclude a number of items from the sale. The list of items she retained provided us with a fascinating glimpse into the furnishings and possessions of the Shrivers' once grand home.

Restoring the house began on January 2, 1996. The work was a grubby, back-breaking, eight to ten hour a day, six day a week undertaking, but it was definitely a labor of love. That winter brought record breaking low temperatures, more than a hundred inches of snow and two major floods that made national news. But the rewards far outweighed the obstacles, because each day brought about new discoveries. In addition to learning more and more about the Shriver family, countless treasures were found within the house - inside walls, underneath fireplace hearths and under floorboards. Numerous artifacts were discovered in the garden as well, including several horse's teeth.

Six bullets found under the floorboards in the garret.

One of the first, and certainly the most exciting, of these finds was discovered in the attic. Learning about the sharpshooters led to uncovering the original loopholes knocked through the garret wall by the Confederates in July, 1863. By chance, while working in the attic, we had to pull up a floorboard directly below one of the two loopholes. Under a 1½" wide crack in the floorboard were six

Civil War cartridges and a number of percussion caps! Three of these bullets were virtually intact; that is, they contained the original paper cartridge with the gunpowder still inside. Two were Confederate .58 caliber Gardner bullets, and one was a Union .58 caliber Minie ball. Inasmuch as these bullets were interchangeable, the Confederates in our garret were obviously using some captured Union ammunition.

Discovering the bullets, of course, meant we had to look beneath *all* the floorboards in the attic. We were surprised, and delighted, to discover a stash of medical supplies. Among these medical supplies was a small ceramic jar containing an ointment made of cubebs. Cubebs are small berries resembling black peppercorns once used to treat stomach ailments including dysentery, the most common ailment among soldiers. We also found an 8" long syringe made entirely of glass, which would have been used to administer the medicine contained within

Medical supplies found hidden under the garret floorboards.

the next find, a 9" high bottle labeled *Lindsay's Blood Searcher* manufactured in Hollidaysburg, Pennsylvania. Although the bottle is clearly marked *patented heart medicine*, forensic analysis of its contents reveals this *miracle cure* to be made of herbal ingredients quite effective in the treatment of dysentery. Today, however, this concoction would be referred to as *snake oil*.

An advertisement in *The Adams Sentinel and General Advertiser*, dated September 12, 1860, described *Lindsay's Blood Searcher* as:

LINDSEY'S IMPROVED BLOOD SEARCHER,
A standard Medicine for the speedy, radical, and
effectual cure of all Diseases arising from
impurity of the Blood.
This medicine has wrought the most miraculous
cures in desperate cases of

Scrofula,	Cancerous formations,
Cutaneous Diseases,	Erysipelas, Boils,
Pimples on the face,	Sore Eyes,
Old, Stubborn Ulcers,	Scald Head,
Tetter affections,	Rheumatic Disorders,
Dyspepsia,	Costiveness,
Jaundice,	Salt Rheum,
Mercurial Diseases,	General Debility,
Liver Complaint,	Loss of Appetite,
Low Spirits,	Foul Stomach,

Female Complaints, and all Diseases having their origin
in an impure state of the Blood.

Perhaps these medical supplies were hidden under a garret floorboard by one soldier stashing it away in safekeeping for a wounded comrade lying elsewhere in the house. Although meant to be utilized at a later time, the medicine, obviously, was never retrieved.

There were hundreds of objects found inside the house during the restoration. The most historically relevant and noteworthy were the unspent bullets and the medical supplies. The most precious and poignant discovery of all, however, was one leather, high-top child's shoe found in the ceiling of the northeast bedroom on the second floor. According to an old custom, placing a shoe within the wall of a house during construction would bring good luck to the family that would live in the home. Thus, more than likely, this shoe belonged to Sadie or Mollie and was put there by George and Hettie Shriver more than 135 years earlier.

Shoe found hidden inside a
wall of the Shrivers' home.

Other items found throughout the house are far too numerous to recount. Among the hundreds of objects found were corset stays, straight razors, toys, dolls, tardiness slips and holy cards from St. Francis School (located just a block away), two gas pipes and two gas lamps, bottles for medicine and for liquor, paper dolls, a roller skate, two rat traps, clothes, photographs, letters, jewelry, a chamber pot lid, newspapers and several pairs of eyeglasses. These items serve as a time capsule representing all the families who, for more than a century, called this house their *home*.

When Daniel Trimmer purchased Hettie's home in 1866, he and his neighbor and business partner, Henry Garlach, placed the following advertisement in the *Gettysburg Compiler* on July 3rd of that same year:

TO THE PUBLIC.
GARLACH & TRIMMER,
Cabinet Maker, Undertakers and
Chair Makers

Ten years later, on August 3, 1876, an advertisement in the same paper read:

The February 22, 1887 *Gettysburg Compiler* lists one particular lot of ground for sale which included a "two story brick house . . . Shop 14 by 65. . ." owned by Daniel Trimmer. Although Mr. Trimmer and Mr. Garlach were no longer business partners, Mr. Trimmer, it appears, used George's ten-pin alley for his cabinet-making shop and the saloon as his show room. Consequently, neither the saloon nor the ten-pin alley were ever used for their intended purposes.

~~~ ~~~ ~~~

In 2006, a forensics expert from the Crime Scene Unit of the Niagara Falls Police Department, using a latent blood reagent, uncovered evidence of the presence of blood in the attic. After making the room as dark as possible, Det. Lt. Nick Paonessa saturated the attic floorboards with Bluestar® Forensic reagent, focusing on the areas immediately below the two loopholes through which Confederates were known to be shot during the Battle of Gettysburg. The results were astonishing! In an area roughly six feet in diameter beneath each loophole, the reagent produced a bright green luminescence indicating the presence of trace amounts of hemoglobin still imbedded within the wood; in other words, they detected the presence of blood! Numerous bright spots, ranging in size from ¼" to 1½" in diameter, revealed evidence of blood splatter on the brick wall surrounding the loopholes; the shadow of a wiping motion, obviously produced by someone cleaning up the blood-laden scene, was also clearly visible. This scientific evidence corroborated the accounts of Confederates being shot while in the Shrivers' attic during the battle, as reported by their neighbors, James Pierce and Henry Rupp, more than one hundred and forty years earlier.

~~~ ~~~ ~~~

We faced many challenges during the restoration of the Shriver House. The most difficult challenge was to find photographs of the Shriver family. Although we had searched for several years, one day in early 2002, a guest who toured the house asked if she could help; genealogy was her passion. Utilizing state of the art computer technology, she located Hettie Shriver Pittenturf's great-great-granddaughter, Anne Nemeth-Barath, a retired school teacher who lived about an hour and a half away in Winchester, Virginia. After numerous telephone conversations and emails, Anne and her husband, Dan, came to visit. Fortunately, Anne was also dedicated to preserving her family's history and brought with her a wealth of information including her family Bible containing birth, death and marriage records - some in Hettie Shriver's own handwriting! She also shared numerous family anecdotes that had been passed down through relatives.

Anne rummaged through a wooden trunk that had belonged to her great-grandmother, Lillie Mae (Hettie's daughter). There she found a long-forgotten album Lillie had filled with photographs of family and friends, each person identified by name! In the back of the album was a small compartment where tiny keepsakes could be tucked away. Although she had been in possession of this album for many years, Anne had never bothered to look inside this compartment. To her surprise she found four photographs Lillie had secreted away many years earlier. The first was a photo of two little girls about seven and five years of age, Sadie and Mollie. The second was of Hettie; based on the style of her dress it was probably taken sometime in the 1870s. There was a photograph of Daniel Free Pittenturf who was Hettie's second husband and Lillie's father. The last was of a finely dressed, extremely handsome young man, George Washington Shriver.

For years we were obsessed with finding so little as a single photograph of any one of the Shriver family members, never dreaming we would encounter *all of them* at the same time on the very same day. After six years of telling the story of the Shriver family many hundreds of times to thousands of visitors, we now had faces to go along with that story, making it all the more real and personal. In all the years we have been associated with the *Shriver House Museum* this was, without a doubt, the most thrilling and rewarding day of all!

From the time George and Hettie built their dream home in 1860, six families have called this house their home. But how many people have walked these same floors and climbed these same stairs without knowing the story of the young family who built the house and the history that took place within these walls? Now, for the first time, their story has been told.

Shriver vs. Schriver

Since the beginning of our nation, immigrants to America have frequently changed their names for a variety of reasons. This happened in some cases when immigration officials misunderstood foreign pronunciations and wrote down what they thought they heard. In other cases, changes were made by the immigrants themselves to create a more American sounding name.

George Washington Shriver's great-grandfather, Jacob Schreiber, was born in Beirach, Germany in the early 1700s.

He came to the New World by ship, arriving in Baltimore Harbor in the 1730s. Their surname, spelled *Schreiber*, is the German word for *writer*. Desiring to sound more American, they changed the spelling of their name from *Schreiber* to the more Anglicized version, either *Shriver* or *Schriver*.

Both spellings, *Shriver* and *Schriver*, are used when researching the history of the family. When the museum initially opened it was called the *Schriver House Museum* because it seemed their name was more often found spelled with a "c." This is the spelling Tillie Pierce used in her book, *At Gettysburg or What a Girl Saw and Heard of the Battle*. After additional research, this initial impression proved to be incorrect as more documents were found without the "c," and at least one document spelled it both ways. When Mollie Shriver was nineteen years old she had occasion to sign a legal document twice on the same page. One signature appears as *Mollie Shriver* (without the "c"), while the second is spelled *Mollie Schriver* (with the "c").

In 2005 the name was formally changed from *Schriver House Museum* to *Shriver House Museum*.

Timeline

1730s

Jacob Shriver emigrates from Germany; settles in Anne Arundel County, Maryland. Lewis P., one of Jacob's nine children, is born in 1750 and, after serving in the Revolutionary War, relocates to south central Pennsylvania.

1786

Lewis P. Shriver establishes a farm and builds a 36' x 20' log cabin along Marsh Creek. In 1790 builds a large stone farmhouse. His farm includes a small orchard, granary, stone springhouse, large bank barn, grist mill, blacksmith shop and weaver's shop. He is growing wheat, oats, rye and corn. Two stillhouses produce substantial quantities of gin, rye whiskey and apple brandy.

1800

Lewis P. Shriver receives the deed for 211 acres, 48 perches of land he purchased from the Manor of the Maske (Wm. Penn's descendants) for £102, 6 shillings, 10 pence.

1836

Hettie is born to Jacob and Sarah Weikert on March 7th.

George W. is born to George Lewis and Mary Shriver on July 27th.

1847

George Lewis Shriver owns a 211 acre farm and a 222 acre farm.

1848

George Lewis Shriver owns a 211 acre farm.

Christian Shriver (George's brother) now owns a 222 acre farm.

1849

Isaac Shriver (George's brother) purchases 230 acres of land in the vicinity of his father's and brother's farms.

1852

George Lewis Shriver dies. At the age of sixteen, George W. Shriver inherits the family farm.

1854

Maria Shriver (George's sister) marries Emmanuel Weikert (Hettie's brother).

1855

Hettie Weikert marries George W. Shriver on January 23rd.

Sarah Louisa, *Sadie*, is born to George and Hettie Shriver on November 21st.

1857

Mary Margaret, *Mollie*, is born to George and Hettie Shriver on August 13th.

1859

Jacob Emmanuel is born to George and Hettie Shriver on June 4th; Jacob dies at the age of 2 months, 24 days; he was buried in Mt. Joy Lutheran Cemetery.

George Shriver sells 31 acres of his farm for $694.37½.

1860

George and Hettie Shriver purchase a 90' x 140' lot of ground on Baltimore Street. The *Gettysburg Compiler* reports on May 14th: "Mr. Geo. W. Schriver is building a two-story brick residence on Baltimore street, adjoining Mr. James Pierce."

1861

George Shriver sells remaining 180 acres of his farm for $3,420.

The American Civil War begins on April 12th.

George Shriver musters into Cole's Cavalry, Co. C., 1st Potomac Home Brigade, Maryland Cavalry, on September 9th.

1863

Battle of Gettysburg takes place on July 1st, 2nd and 3rd.

Abraham Lincoln dedicates the Soldiers' National Cemetery on November 19th.

George Shriver comes home on a four-day furlough at Christmas.

1864

George Shriver is captured near Rectortown, Virginia, on New Year's Day.

The January 11th edition of the *Gettysburg Compiler* reports Cole's Cavalry's engagement with Mosby's Rangers; George Shriver is listed with the names of those taken prisoner and missing.

George Shriver is promoted from Corporal to Sergeant on January 14th.

Cynthia Powers Pittenturf dies leaving Daniel Pittenturf a widower.

December 12th issue of the *Gettysburg Compiler* reports George Shriver's death on August 25th "whilst in the hands of the rebels" in Andersonville, Georgia.

1866

Hettie Shriver sells her home and one side lot of ground to Daniel Trimmer for $2,100; Hettie retains a 30' lot of ground.

Hettie Shriver marries Daniel Pittenturf on July 19th.

Daniel's three year old son, James, dies on October 7th after falling into a bucket of scalding water.

1867

Lillie Mae is born to Daniel and Hettie Pittenturf on April 17th.

1869

Emma is born to Daniel and Hettie Pittenturf on September 12th; Emma dies 28 days later.

1870

U.S. Census lists Frank Powers Pittenturf (Daniel's son) as living with Solomon and Catherine Powers, his maternal grandparents.

1874

Sadie Shriver dies on November 6th at the age of 18 years, 11 months, 4 days. Sadie is buried in Lot 330, Section A in Evergreen Cemetery.

1878

Mary Fisher Rife Shriver (George's mother) dies at the age of 79 years, 10 months, 3 days.

Mollie Shriver marries William A. Stallsmith on December 1st.

1880

Mollie Shriver dies on July 16th at the age of 22 years, 11 months, 3 days. Mollie is buried in Lot 233, Section G in Evergreen Cemetery.

1885

Lillie Mae Pittenturf marries William Allen Hollebaugh on July 12th.

©1892

Hettie and Daniel Pittenturf move to Harrisburg, Pennsylvania, to live with her daughter, Lillie, and her husband, William Allen Hollebaugh.

1900

Daniel Pittenturf dies on March 17th at the age of 71 in Baltimore, Maryland.

1916

Henrietta Weikert Shriver Pittenturf dies on April 7th at the age of 80 years, 1 month, at the home of her daughter, Lillie, in Washington, D.C. She is buried in Section J, Lot 24, Site 9, Glenwood Cemetery, Washington, D.C.

Bibliography

Works utilized in the preparation of this book are fully cited within the body of the text when first referenced. In addition to these, factual information about the Shrivers has been obtained from a variety of sources, including the National Archives, the Library of Congress, Adams County Historical Society, Emmitsburg Historical Society, Andersonville National Historic Site, birth records, marriage records, real estate records, tax records, census records, obituaries, wills, newspapers, letters, personal interviews, tombstones and army records.

The following works were consulted.

Alleman, Tillie (Pierce). *At Gettysburg, or What a Girl Saw and Heard of the Battle: A True Narrative.* New York: W. Lake Borland, 1889. Gettysburg, PA: Shriver House Museum, 2015 reprint.

Bennett, Gerald R. *Days of Uncertainty and Dread: The Ordeal Endured by the Citizens of Gettysburg.* Self-Published, 1994.

Broadhead, Sarah M. *The Diary of a Lady of Gettysburg, Pennsylvania, From June 15 to July 15, 1863.* Hershey, PA: Gary T. Hawbaker, 2002 reprint.

Buehler, Fannie J. *Recollections of the Rebel Invasion and One Woman's Experience During the Battle of Gettysburg.* Gettysburg, 1896. Hershey, PA: Gary T. Hawbaker, 2002 reprint.

Creighton, Margaret S. *The Colors of Courage, Gettysburg's Forgotten History: Immigrants, Women, and African Americans in the Civil War's Defining Battle.* New York: Basic Books, 2005.

Frassanito, William A. *Early Photography at Gettysburg.* Gettysburg: Thomas Publications, 1995.

McCreary, Albertus. *Gettysburg: A Boy's Experience of the Battle.* McClure's Magazine, vol. 18, no. 33. New York: S.S. McClure Co., July, 1909.

Skelly, Daniel Alexander. *A Boy's Experiences During the Battles of Gettysburg.* Self-Published, 1932.

Slade, Jim and John. Alexander. *Firestorm at Gettysburg: Civilian Voices.* Atglen, PA: Schiffer Publishing Co., 1998.

Styple, William B. *Andersonville: Giving up the Ghost.* Kearney, NJ: Belle Grove Publishing Co., 1996.

Williams, William G. *Days of Darkness: The Gettysburg Civilians.* Shippensburg, PA: White Mane Books, 2001 (orig. 1986).

Photo Credit

Dan and Anne Nemeth-Barath, front cover, pp. 2, 3, 4, 86, 89.
Amy Lindenberger, p. 5.
Del Gudmestad, back cover, pp. 6, 9, 21, 72, 95 (top), 96, 97 99.
William R. Marcus, p. 84.
Donny Thompson, back cover, pp. 8, 11, 13, 15, 95 (bottom).
Darryl Wheeler, back cover (author).
Adams County Historical Society, Gettysburg, PA, pp. 35, 38.
Gettysburg National Military Park, p. 77.
Heide Presse, p. 90.
No source identified, p. 39.

Although much has been accomplished in bringing the Shriver House back to its original appearance, it remains, nonetheless, a restoration in progress. George and Hettie's home has been restored privately; no funds are received from any foundations or government agencies for its preservation. Entrance fees paid by visitors to tour the *Shriver House Museum* help to preserve and improve this unique part of our heritage.